Shrimp Country

University Press of Florida

Florida A&M University, Tallahassee

Florida Atlantic University, Boca Raton

Florida Gulf Coast University, Ft. Myers

Florida International University, Miami

Florida State University, Tallahassee

New College of Florida, Sarasota

University of Central Florida, Orlando

University of Florida, Gainesville

University of North Florida, Jacksonville

University of South Florida, Tampa

University of West Florida, Pensacola

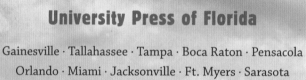

University Press of Florida

Gainesville · Tallahassee · Tampa · Boca Raton · Pensacola
Orlando · Miami · Jacksonville · Ft. Myers · Sarasota

Shrimp Country

Recipes and Tales
from the Southern Coasts

Anna Marlis Burgard

21 20 19 18 17 16   6 5 4 3 2 1

The University Press of Florida is the scholarly
publishing agency for the State University System
of Florida, comprising Florida A&M University,
Florida Atlantic University, Florida Gulf Coast
University, Florida International University,
Florida State University, New College of Florida,
University of Central Florida, University of
Florida, University of North Florida, University
of South Florida, and University of West Florida.

University Press of Florida
15 Northwest 15th Street
Gainesville, FL 32611-2079
http://www.upf.com

A record of cataloging-in-publication data is
available from the Library of Congress.
ISBN 978-0-8130-6294-5

All photos are by the author unless otherwise
noted.

Pages ii–iii: Parallel parking in Fulton, Texas.

Following page: A still morning along Mosquito
Creek, Little St. Simons Island, Georgia.

For the trawler crews,
the chefs,
and the marine biologists
—storytellers, all

Contents

Introduction

The Laguna Madre shimmered in the September sun as I crossed the Queen Isabella Causeway onto South Padre Island. I headed straight for the southernmost point that faces Mexico's shore, just eight miles away. The Brazos Santiago Pass—"The Arms of St. James"— bounds the island here; the thirty-foot-deep channel is blessedly calm and welcoming after the open seas, and so was named in honor of Spain's patron saint. I climbed up on the jetty's rocks and looked across the water to Brazos Island, where a handful of old wooden cottages were lit like a Hopper painting. A man using shrimp to lure fish fed his smaller catches to a cat stationed next to him. Jetty's Bait Stand, with its primary colors, handwritten sign for beer, and wind-flapped flag, was a perfect addition to the scene. I took it all in like a desiccated sponge reanimated by the salt water it was born to.

The sun's last rays strike a bait shop on South Padre Island, Texas.

I'd driven for eight days from Spokane, Washington's high desert through Idaho, Utah, Colorado, New Mexico, and much of Texas—including a postapocalyptic stretch marked by "nodding donkey" pumpjacks, dried-up draws, tumbleweed, and a hotel where the clerk greeted me with a drawled "I didn't think we had any *women* staying here tonight." There were beautiful sites, too, along the way, including Utah's Arches National Park red rock country and Georgia O'Keeffe's Ghost Ranch. But I'm a sea-and-sand girl, so a week straight of arid skies, smoked meat, and eighteen-wheelers had just about done me in.

Twenty-four hundred miles is a long way to travel for a nice view and a salty breeze, though, and as much as I love the beach, this was no vacation. The real driving—more than three thousand more miles—as well as the work and fun—was about to begin. With my wheels aimed for the entire Gulf of Mexico and southern Atlantic coasts, I was on a mission to wrangle shrimp recipes from trawler captains' families, food truck masters, diner cooks, and award-winning chefs alike. Along the way, I would hear epic tales, see strange and beautiful places, and sample some of the best food America has to offer. It was a tough job, but someone had to do it.

Genesis

My first shrimp memory is of a mountain of succulent, sunset-colored beauties on our table during a family vacation on Emerald Isle, North Carolina. Dad steamed them with boiling spices and beer, and we grabbed handfuls and greedily peeled and ate until all that remained were shells and soaked newspaper. Decades later, I visited Tybee Island, Georgia; my first image of the island was its green-netted shrimp trawlers lined up along the docks beneath the Lazaretto Creek Bridge. I happened upon an available house where the lighthouse would shine into my living room at night, and spontaneously decided to move there. For seven transformative years I watched the trawlers head out to sea at dawn, their lights twinkling against rose and lavender clouds, and then return to the docks in the afternoon, trailed by gulls and dolphins. The boats provide great atmosphere even when still, with their groaning

Tybee Island, Georgia is no place for suits and ties; guys abandon their business brains by decorating this marsh bush.

ropes straining against the docks in high winds and their lowered nets spread out in neighboring Cockspur Island's channel like an open-armed "welcome home."

The company of captains, marine biologists, and folks who cast nets off their creek docks was part of what hooked me: It's the laid-back vibe of these places where people work hard, but still seem to enjoy life without a lot of complications. During my stint on the island I naturally ate a lot of shrimp. Tybee's chefs are among the best I've encountered on any island, anywhere, so the variety and quality were a pure delight. I also tinkered with my own recipes, including a shrimp scampi I'd been cooking for years, changing it here and there as I went—but its final incarnation was born on Tybee (see page 203 for the recipe).

I reluctantly left my Lowcountry island for a position in Washington—the eastern high desert part of the state. I was living within sight of the Spokane River (and earshot of it during snowmelt), but was a four-hour drive from the coast. Rivers, no matter how big and mighty, just aren't the same as wide-open water, the expansiveness of it, its salt coming into your lungs. I drove to the Puget Sound islands over and over again until I finally figured out that islands are a passion for me, not just places to land for a week here and there. So I did the rational thing: I quit my job, and dove into studying and experiencing as many water-framed spots of land as I could. I've now visited more than one hundred islands in twenty-five states; a large percentage of those are in the South, so along the way I've dined on shrimp in every Gulf and southern Atlantic state from South Padre Island, Texas, to Stumpy Point, North Carolina. It seemed only natural to gather some of these recipes and the stories that surround them, given that I've been making books since I was about seven.

A Perfect Food

Shrimp is an ideal ingredient: It's delicious, low-calorie, and high-protein, and it provides vitamins, minerals, and omega-3 fatty acids. It's mild enough that hundreds of recipes can be built around it, but flavorful enough to be eaten on its own, right out of the shell. It pairs well with both spicy and sweet ingredients and can be fried, sautéed, steamed, broiled, or grilled. It can be served on pasta, polenta, grits, biscuits, rice, or cornbread (even waffles, in a stretch). It's at home in informal dishes served out on the deck, or as the refined centerpiece of a damask-and-silver dinner.

The summer season on Tybee Island kicks off with the Beach Bum Parade in May—an island-long battle with aquatic ammunition.

I could eat shrimp every day, and often do, for stretches. I've an ode to the critters waiting to be written, illustrating and celebrating their virtues. Shrimp are in most salt waters, which means maritime nations around the world have their own takes on shrimp recipes. Americans consume a billion pounds a year in a wide array of preparations. The boats haul 'em in, and home cooks and chefs transform them into heirloom dishes like scampi and Newburg as well as regional classics like bog, perloo, and mull. Every shore town has its favorite dishes concocted from local ingredients and immigrant culinary traditions: Cuban shrimp enchiladas in Key West, Greek shrimp saganaki in Tarpon Springs, African shrimp gumbo in New Orleans, Mexican chipotle shrimp on South Padre Island, and a shrimp bisque in Charleston that's a nod to its French Huguenot heritage.

I'm of the *bonne femme* school—in the manner of a good housewife, food prepared in a simple style—influenced by my mother, who cooked for eight or more people every day for decades. My father came to cooking and baking later in life and, being German, was more a "letter of the law" man who followed complex recipes precisely. I'm more a "spirit of the law" type, preferring to wing it and invent dishes on the fly,

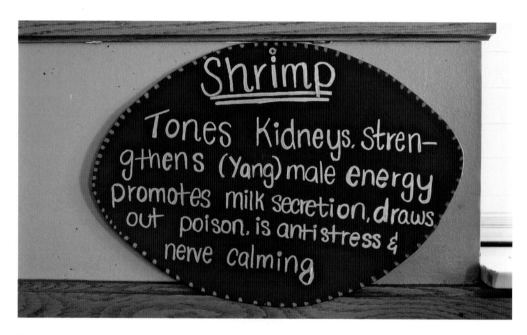

The benefits of eating shrimp as understood by Chinese medicine, The Great Machipongo Clam Shack, Nassawadox, Virginia.

Facing: Cherry Point Seafood's office door, Rockville, South Carolina.

although I started cooking from recipes when I was 13, when my mother went back to college. Dad bought the Betty Crocker Recipe File from the television commercial and set me loose a couple nights each week. I'd always liked to cook, and also serve guests, so I was the natural alternate from the siblings still at home.

Every chef, like every artist, is part magpie, so each recipe is a kind of culinary nest, with bits gathered from family traditions, local ingredients, ethnic influences—even what's sittin' in the fridge that needs to be used up. Recipe development is a creative process like any other: Flavors blend like notes in music and colors in paintings to create the compelling whole. But of all the main ingredients out there, nothing is more versatile, or prettier, than shrimp.

Commercial Shrimping

Every epic journey needs a knowledgeable guide; Dante had Virgil, Aeneas had Sybil. I had marine biologist Tony Reisinger, who met me on South Padre Island on that September kick-off day. Tony knows the Gulf and southern Atlantic coasts like the back of his hands, having lived on islands in Georgia, Florida, and Texas; his specialization is shrimp and their harvesting, and his knowledge is encyclopedic. He taught me about counts (basically, the smaller the number, the fewer shrimp per pound—so "colossals" are a 10-count, where medium shrimp might be more like a 25) as well as kinds: whites in the Carolinas and Georgia; Florida's rock shrimp, pinks ("hoppers"), and royal red varieties; Texas's brownies.

Tony also informed me about the habits of shrimp and the behaviors of shrimpers through numerous colorful stories from the industry's history, not to mention introductions to key characters. During shrimping's heyday through the 1970s or so, trawlers were lined up four and five deep at the docks; now, nationwide, there remain only a few thousand, from the day shrimpers that stay close to bays and creeks to the guys who head out to the open water for weeks at a time. Diesel fuel costs, competition from low-priced Asian farmed shrimp, oil spills, skyrocketing real estate values along the coasts, and other obstacles have forced many, if not most, of the generations-old shrimping families out of the business. Captains have made adjustments to their boats since the mid-twentieth century, including outfitting their rigs with refrigerated holds, adding TEDs (turtle excluder devices) to their nets to protect

Headers at work on the haul at Hobo Seafood's dock in Swanquarter, North Carolina.

marine species, and equipping themselves with GPS systems, but in their essences, the boats, the business, and the crews are much as they were a hundred years ago.

I spoke with captains in each of the coastal states—a feat in itself, according to some, given their generally cautious and sometimes cantankerous ranks. I met a few who, based on first impressions, honestly might have given me a scare on a lonely street, but I found them universally friendly and engaging. The nature of their physical work, and the tender ages at which they begin in the business—generally forcing them to forgo most conventional education—can present a pretty rough exterior, but they're epic storytellers and incredibly hardworking men. Their omens, their recipes, their tattoos, their scars, the descriptions of strange items hauled up along with the shrimp, the storms they've survived—these mariners straddle the ancient and modern worlds.

Of course the trawlers aren't the only way to pull shrimp to shore. Folks cast nets from their Georgia docks, with their boots ankle deep in South Carolina's pluff mud creeks, or from their skiffs a little farther out into bays in Texas. Along Alabama's Point Clear coast, the shrimp might come to you as they swim to shore in the middle of a summer night during a "jubilee" event (for more on this, see page 64). A good haul is shared with the neighbors and cooked up using recipes immortalized on stained index cards, rumpled loose-leaf sheets, and in the closely guarded mental files of some of the South's culinary artists—whether James Beard Award–winning chefs or someone's beloved grandmother.

Shrimp Country is my way of honoring the shrimping communities through the joy of their soul-fueling foods and stories. It's a portrait of southern coastal America through a culinary lens. Kick off your shoes, roll up your sleeves, and dig in!

Cast net shrimping along Church Creek's mud banks, Wadmalaw Island, South Carolina.

one

Shrimp Preparation Basics

There are hundreds upon hundreds of ways to prepare shrimp; every southern coastal restaurant has its way to lure in customers with tasty takes, and every coastal family has their favorite way of cooking them. Trawler captains and their families often make a shrimp gravy over rice; folks catching them with cast nets off their docks are just as likely to quickly fry them up in cornmeal or boil them with some spices. That's the beauty of shrimp—you can eat them steamed plain as day or dressed up to the nines with glamorous sauces. Here are some basic rules and tips on boiling, steaming, frying, and grilling your shrimp.

Photo by Charity Burggraaf.

Live oak trees and shrimp trawlers are common presences in South Carolina's Lowcountry.

RULE #1 Wild-caught shrimp taste better, are less processed, and offer you more variety for different dishes. Our Gulf and Southern Atlantic waters provide whites, browns, pinks, royal reds, and rock shrimp, each with their own flavor. Royal reds are the mildest, caught in deep, cold waters, and are generally broiled briefly with butter and nothing else. Browns have the most flavor and hold up better in dishes like jambalaya, where you want to still taste the shrimp through all the spices.

RULE #2 Shrimp cook quickly and get tough if overcooked. They're very helpful, though, and will tell you by their opacity and curling up when they're done. Remember that, as with all foods, they will continue to cook after you take them off the heat.

RULE #3 Shrimp shells (or "hulls," as shrimpers call them) are not garbage. You make shrimp stock from them, which is especially flavorful if you buy head-on shrimp and throw the shells and heads into the pot. You'll use this stock for your grits, rice, stews, and whatever else you want a deeper flavor for than water can provide. Use it like chicken stock, but for seafood dishes.

RULE #4 It doesn't matter if shrimp are frozen when you buy them—the trawler crews put them on ice or into deep freezes as soon as they catch them. Unless you're buying from day shrimpers from their decks or close to them, the shrimp has been frozen. If you're inland or not at a seafood market, if it isn't frozen, it's been thawed— and will lose flavor rapidly. You want shrimp to smell like the sea, not like something your nose snaps back from. Look for "I.Q.F." on the label for the freshest shrimp on the market: "individually quick frozen."

If you're freezing fresh-caught shrimp, head them, leaving the shells on, then rinse under cold water. Pack them with ice in well-sealed containers in amounts that are right for how you'll cook them later (1 to 2 pounds for recipes, more for feasts if you have a freezer big enough). Add water up to about an inch from the container's rim to allow for expansion during freezing.

RULE #5 The lower the count per pound, the bigger the shrimp. A 26/30 count is the median; a 10-count shrimp is colossal.

RULE #6 Most people will eat ½ to 1 pound of shrimp if they're peeled.

The Ten Commandments
of Shrimp

(Casting aside Leviticus 11:9–12)

1 Thou shalt purchase wild American shrimp when it's available.

2 Thou shalt honor thy shrimp fishermen, who risk their lives bringing the delicacy to shore.

3 Thou shalt not throw away shrimp shells but shall make and freeze shrimp stock for future recipes.

4 Thou shalt not overcook thy shrimp until it becomes a flavorless piece of rubber.

5 Thou shalt not throw away leftover steamed shrimp but shall make any of the scores of recipes that showcase it (within a day or so).

6 Thou shalt delight in down-home regional shrimp dishes including bog, mull, perloo, and gumbo.

7 Thou shalt not demean shrimp with thy poorly made grits or drown them in flavorless sauces.

8 Thou shalt share thy bounty with friends and neighbors when thou catchest more than a teaser haul off thy dock.

9 Thou shalt not turn thy nose up at frozen shrimp but shall understand that most trawlers freeze shrimp immediately after catching them to keep them fresh.

10 Thou shalt bow down and thank the Lord for shrimp fresh off the boat in all its jewel-toned goodness.

Grace Chapel, Rockville, South Carolina.

Steamed or Boiled Shrimp

There are only a couple rules for boiling shrimp; beyond that, everyone's aunt knows the "best" way, just like every other neighborhood dad knows the best way to grill chicken. The most important thing to remember is that they're less forgiving than other meats and will become tough and flavorless if you overcook them. Boil or steam them for 3 to 5 minutes, just until they turn pink and curl up—how big they are will determine how long they'll need. Once they're pink, dump them into a colander or the sink and run cold water over them, or throw a bag of ice into the pot. The cold shock stops the cooking and also helps the shells come off more easily, according to some.

When my dad cooked shrimp for a newspaper-on-the-picnic-table, beers-in-the-cooler feast, he poured a can of beer into the huge enamelware pot and used Old Bay as the seasoning (because we grew up in Maryland) sprinkled on the shrimp in their rack. If you're using the shrimp for a recipe, you'll want to be careful about adding too much spice.

Another rule of thumb is that you'll get between two thirds and half the weight of shrimp after shelling them (depending on if they have heads on and what size they are—larger shrimp yield more meat per shrimp versus shell weight). So, take that into account when shopping, estimating ½ (in a prepared dish) to 1 pound (peel-and-eat) per guest.

Some poach the shrimp in just enough water to cover them; others boil the shrimp in as much as 4 quarts of water per pound. If you opt to boil, add the shrimp after the water is boiling, cover the pot, take them off the heat until they're cooked through, then drain.

Here are some additional "secrets" I've heard over the years. Bear in mind that each and every tip would likely be refuted as often as supported by other "experts"!

- The WD-40 Approach: Add ½ stick butter or ¼ cup Italian salad dressing to the boiling water to make peeling the shells easier.

- The Salem Test: If they're floating, they're cooked. Scoop them out as soon as they rise to the top.

- Soup It Up: After the water's boiling, add a sliced onion, a few celery ribs, garlic cloves, bay leaves, sliced lemons, and peppercorns, then add the shrimp.

- Afterthought: Toss the seafood boil spice on the shrimp after they're cooked because the salt in the blend makes the shells stick, and you can control the spice level if some people prefer milder flavor while others want the spice coating each shrimp.

Fried Shrimp

Lots of coastal folks say their favorite way to eat shrimp is fried without a lot of fuss, just a quick dredge through cornmeal or flour, nothing that takes too much away from the flavor of the shrimp itself. But even a cooking method that seems like a no brainer has old pro tips. I learned some of these by *not* minding my own business while communing with tomato pie at Stono Market on Johns Island in South Carolina; my ears pivoted toward a conversation about a recent cast net catch off a private dock. I followed up with my table neighbor, Michael Peterson, to add some of the following suggestions to my growing collection. As a lifelong Lowcountry resident, he knows his shrimp.

TIPS

✦ Bears repeating: Guests will eat between ½ and 1 pound of fried shrimp each unless they're being passed rather than served while seated, in which case they're likely to eat less.

✦ Use oils with a high smoke point and a neutral flavor. Your best bets are canola, safflower, and peanut, but peanut oil has a deeper flavor—and if you're cooking for a crowd you will want to avoid it because of allergies.

✦ Keep the shrimp—and its batter or dredging ingredients—in the freezer for an hour before you fry them.

✦ For more kick, before they coat the shrimp, some people marinate them for an hour in a combination of Worcestershire, soy, and hot sauces and Italian dressing, or whatever floats your boat. This way the flavor comes from the shrimp rather than a sauce you dip them into.

✦ Some people dress up their cornmeal crust with dashes of garlic and onion powders and lemon pepper seasoning.

✦ If you batter your shrimp, dredge them in flour first, shaking excess free, then dip in an egg and buttermilk mixture (maybe with a splash of hot sauce or a little mustard), and dredge in the cornmeal. Some will tell you not to use egg or water before dredging the shrimp in flour, fish fry mix, or what have you—that the shrimp are lighter without the binder.

Gerald's Pig and Shrimp gives a nod to the trawling heritage of Tybee Island, Georgia. The metal shrimp is formed from forks and spoons.

❖ Shake excess cornmeal or flour free by tossing the shrimp in a colander or mesh sieve. A "breading box" or basket can also be used.

❖ Pour oil 3 inches deep into a Dutch oven or other deep-sided pot, if not using a deep fryer.

❖ Various coastal experts list the ideal temperature range for deep frying between 325 and 375°F. The oil is ready when you sprinkle a pinch of flour on top and it sizzles on contact. Basically, the higher the temperature the less oil that will saturate the batter. Dredged but not battered shrimp may do better at the lower temperature.

❖ Fry shrimp in small batches; don't crowd them in a pan or deep fryer basket.

❖ As soon as the shrimp float to the top, lift them out with a slotted spoon or sieve. Drain on paper towels or old paper grocery bags.

❖ If you plan to use the oil a second time, strain it through a coffee filter once it's cooled and keep it sealed in the refrigerator. A third use is not recommended.

Captain Cook

Captain Barry Woods, the *Island Girl*, Fernandina Beach, Florida

Crews that are out at sea for weeks at a time eat what's fresh, and while shrimpers haul in their share of bycatch (the flounder and other small fish that also get scooped up by the nets), they most often eat shrimp boiled in the very salt water the critters called home or fried, with variations on a shrimp and sausage gravy that's a favorite on trawlers all along the Gulf and southern Atlantic coasts. The captains I've spoken with each have their favorite way of cooking it, prepared by look and feel, with few measurements beyond "a handful" and other old-school amounts.

Captain Barry Woods prides himself on his version. Woods was "borned" on my old haunt, Tybee Island—which he pronounced "Taahbee," forcing me to ask him to repeat himself three times before I got it (tabby is a lime and oyster shell material used like stucco on coastal Georgia structures, which is part of what threw me). He was raised by a shrimper, and was pulling coin

Captain Woods indicates the size of the onions for his recipe.

as a header ("beheader" is a more apt title) on his father's boat, the *Elizabelle*, when he was six. He knows shrimp—from finding where they're "buried up" to hiring skilled strikers to pull in the nets and get the "flickerin' and flippin' prawnies" into bushel baskets, and then selling them at market and directly to chefs.

In between watching the weather, navigating to the wily shrimp, and working with the crew once a catch is hauled in, Woods cooks up his gravy. Within a few minutes of meeting him on Amelia Island and my describing this book, he took a stand: "I've been offered lotsa money for one of my recipes, but I don't think I'll ever give it up." About forty-five minutes later, though, after we'd talked awhile about Tybee and how "it don't matter what the deal is, you gotta be around that salt air," he decided I needed to learn how to make shrimp gravy, so he talked and gestured his way through his recipe:

"Coat your shrimp in nothin' but flour—fry 'em in enough peanut oil just to turn 'em over 'til they're brown, and keep the dribblins. Fry up salt pork, cut up in little bitsy pieces, with veggies in the dribblins. Butter's always a little bit in there, and this 'n' that, and Worcestershire sauce. Fry two cut-up links of sausage in it all, then add the shrimp back in, and put it on some rice. The only vegetables I use are onions, bell pepper, and celery. Of course Cajuns cook theirs up with boudin, but you can use different sausage, any kind you like. Just have to balance it all so you taste the shrimp—not too much rice or green pepper or celery."

Without knowing what the "this 'n' that" is, or the real amounts, I'm sure I'll never truly make Woods's version, but, no doubt, this'll "make your tongue slap your brains out." ✤

Shrimp Stock

When you know that a third of the money you pay for shrimp is spent on the shells (and sometimes heads), you learn to get more value out of what others might discard. Shrimp stock makes dishes more delicious, just like chicken stock does. Freeze the shells after you peel the shrimp if you don't have enough to make stock, and wait until they add up.

A basic stock is made from the shells brought to a boil in water (roughly twice as many cups of water as there were pounds of shrimp) and simmered with parsley, onion, celery, and peppercorns. Let it simmer for an hour or so, strain the liquid through a metal sieve, then freeze the stock if not using right away. If the heads are included, pinch them so the fats drain into the stock.

Some people sauté the shells first in a little olive oil until they turn orange-pink, then add a couple cups of water and some wine (depending on how many shells they have), let everything simmer for an hour or so, then strain the liquid.

One burner, one pot, water drawn from the ocean to cook shrimp just hauled in: the simplicity of life at sea aboard the *Gray Ghost*, Engelhard, North Carolina.

Facing: Freshly rinsed shrimp at Cherry Point Seafood, Rockville, South Carolina.

Grilled or Baked Shrimp

Grilling shrimp is risky business. Grill heats vary, types and sizes of shrimp cook on different schedules, skewers burn, certain marinades catch flame easily. The four basic rules to remember when grilling are:

1 Use a clean, well-oiled grill. Shrimp are delicate critters—make sure your grill is well scrubbed and oiled so you don't lose pieces of them to sticking.

2 Again, don't overcook. In general, shrimp should be grilled no longer than 1 minute or so on each side if shelled (as with marinated shrimp), 2 minutes if the shells are still on (which offers a richer flavor, and keeps them moist). Cooking time depends on how hot your coals or flames are; shrimp will be opaque and/or pink when they're cooked through. Instead of turning the shrimp, you can also cover them with foil—they cook in about 3 minutes this way, and retain more moisture from the steaming (but check them after 2 minutes).

3 Soak kebab skewers for an hour so they won't burn. Remember to leave enough room when you're threading them with shrimp and veggies to be able to grab hold for turning without burning yourself. Thread the shrimp through both the tail and head ends so they don't flop around when you flip the skewers.

4 Pair shrimp with vegetables that will cook at the same rate—split cherry tomatoes and zucchini or squash slices work well; onions and potatoes, if not thinly sliced, will remain raw at the center. Keep the sizes proportional to the shrimp.

Other points to consider:

✤ Don't use the same plate you had the raw shrimp on to serve the cooked shrimp.

✤ As an alternate to marinade, try brushing shelled shrimp with olive oil, then seasoning them with dried oregano (or other spices) and salt and pepper.

✤ If you're serving shell-on shrimp, remember to give your guests a way to clean off their hands, even if just paper towels (but washcloths are much nicer).

✤ Avoid some hassles by baking the shrimp instead. Place the seasoned shrimp in a single layer on a greased, rimmed baking pan or dish. Bake at 325°F for 10 to 12 minutes for medium shrimp, a bit longer for larger shrimp. Turn the shrimp halfway through, and check on them a couple minutes before you think they'll be done. Or, try roasting them shell on with a little sugar and seafood boil spice sprinkled on top in a 450°F oven for 4 to 5 minutes.

two

Shrimp Cocktail Dips

I can't tell you how many coastal (and inland) restaurants I've been to over the past few years; I've visited forty-five of the states, including every one with a coastline, and more than one hundred islands. So I've seen a lot of menus, and I remain puzzled by how shrimp cocktail is trapped in this midcentury presentation of bland shrimp paired with the traditional ketchup and horseradish sauce. I thought it would be fun to take a look at shrimp dips in a different way—to gather the many accompaniment sauces I've encountered, whether drizzled, pooled, or dolloped, to offer tasty alternatives to the tomato sauce. Of course I still love regular ol' cocktail sauce—it's just time it had some competition. So whether you've fried, steamed, or grilled up a batch of shrimp, here are some ways to liven things up.

Loblolly pine catkins along Boneyard Beach, Ossabaw Island, Georgia.

29

Classic Cocktail Sauce

Some folks use vinegar instead of lemon juice for this recipe; there are many ways to put your signature on it, but this is a good basic combination.

Makes about 1/2 cup

INGREDIENTS

½ cup ketchup

2 tablespoons prepared grated horseradish

3 tablespoons fresh lemon juice

A few shakes of hot sauce, if desired

½ teaspoon Worcestershire sauce

PROCESS

Combine all the ingredients in a bowl; cover and refrigerate for at least 1 hour.

Roasted Red Pepper Aioli

Chef Matthew Raiford, The Hunting Lodge | Little St. Simons Island, Georgia

Chef Raiford served this sauce with his Fried Green Tomatoes (see recipe, page 230) when I visited; it's also yummy with fried shrimp, and because it's mild, it would pair well with shrimp grilled with spices.

Makes about 3/4 cup

INGREDIENTS

½ cup roasted red peppers, patted dry if from a jar

¼ cup mayonnaise

¼ teaspoon salt

¼ teaspoon freshly ground black pepper

PROCESS

In a food processor, puree all the ingredients until smooth; cover and chill for at least 1 hour.

Creamy Cocktail Dip

This sauce is one of those quick and easy "ingredients on hand" recipes.

Makes about 3/4 cup

INGREDIENTS

½ cup mayonnaise

¼ cup sour cream

2 cloves garlic, minced (2 teaspoons)

2 teaspoons fresh lemon juice

½ teaspoon seafood boil spice (or more if
 more heat is desired)

PROCESS

Combine all the ingredients in a bowl;
cover and refrigerate for at least 1 hour.

Rémoulade

Chef Fred Neuville, Fat Hen | Johns Island, South Carolina

Rémoulade is a go-to sauce for po'boys and many other southern dishes. Chef Neuville served his along with his family's Pickled Shrimp (see recipe, page 49), but you can use this on sandwiches and as a dip for fried shrimp—or whatever else your tastebuds desire.

Makes about 2 cups

INGREDIENTS

1 cup whole-grain mustard

½ cup mayonnaise

¼ cup ketchup

1 tablespoon seafood boil spice

1 teaspoon cayenne pepper

1 teaspoon fresh lemon juice

1 teaspoon fresh orange juice

1 tablespoon chopped fresh parsley

1 tablespoon chopped chives

2 cloves roasted garlic, made into a paste
 (1 to 2 teaspoons)

Salt and freshly ground black pepper
 to taste

PROCESS

Combine all the ingredients in a bowl.
Taste, adjust salt and pepper, and serve.

Mustard-Lime Dipping Sauce

Chef John Smith, Hemingway's | Santa Rosa Island, Florida

You can find variations of this dip all across Florida, but it's hard to beat the view from Hemingway's.

Makes about 3/4 cup

INGREDIENTS

½ cup mayonnaise
2 tablespoons coarse-ground mustard
Juice of 2 Key limes or 1 regular lime
2 teaspoons honey
½ teaspoon English mustard powder
½ teaspoon Worcestershire sauce
Salt to taste

PROCESS

Combine all the ingredients in a bowl; cover and refrigerate for at least 1 hour.

Tip: It is easier to mix dry mustard powder into wet ingredients if you make it into a paste first; use a little of the honey or lime juice to do so.

Hot Sauce Beurre Blanc

Chef Tory McPhail, Commander's Palace | New Orleans, Louisiana

This is a tasty dip for steamed shrimp and also crabmeat.

Makes 3/4 cup

INGREDIENTS

⅓ cup hot sauce

2 tablespoons minced shallot

6 cloves garlic, minced

¼ cup whipping cream

6 tablespoons unsalted butter, softened

Salt to taste

PROCESS

1 Put the hot sauce, shallot, garlic, and cream in a small saucepan. Over medium heat, simmer until reduced by half, stirring frequently.

2 Slowly whisk the butter, a bit at a time, into the pot, being careful not to let the sauce break up.

3 Strain through a sieve and keep the sauce warm. Add salt.

Greek Tzatziki

Try this classic Greek sauce as a dip for shrimp and tomato kebabs grilled with fresh oregano and olive oil; it's also great on lamb burgers.

Makes about 3/4 cup

INGREDIENTS

½ cup plain Greek yogurt

1 tablespoon mayonnaise

1 teaspoon minced garlic

1 small cucumber, grated, excess water squeezed out

2 dashes salt

PROCESS

Combine all the ingredients in a bowl; cover and refrigerate overnight.

Cajun Red Sauce

Guy Pete | Brownsville, Texas

Guy Pete was a larger-than-life character, one of a handful of Louisiana bayou Cajuns who moved to the Brownsville area in the 1950s or so, opening up new fishing grounds there and down into Mexico. He founded the Brownsville–Port Isabel Shrimpers Association and owned a trawler fleet. At one point, a worker who wanted to unionize the fleet's crews kidnapped him to force the issue. Pete escaped using his pocket knife (a tool no fisherman does without), avoiding the darker fate of being imprisoned in a makeshift plywood coffin the man had waiting for him on Redhead Ridge, a loma (flat-topped rise) that's home to ocelots and other creatures. The man was arrested—and Pete kept the coffin as a souvenir.

Makes about 7 cups

INGREDIENTS

1 (44-ounce) bottle of ketchup

1 (8-ounce) jar of mayonnaise

2 large onions, chopped

1 head of garlic, cloves separated
   and peeled

1 jalapeño pepper, seeded and with
   membranes trimmed

Hot sauce to taste

1 (8-ounce) bottle of club soda

1 teaspoon grated horseradish,
   or to taste

Freshly ground black pepper to taste

PROCESS

1 In a blender, puree the ketchup, mayonnaise, onions, garlic, jalapeño, and hot sauce.

2 While blending, add the club soda and horseradish.

3 Taste and add pepper and more hot sauce as desired.

Tip: You could halve this recipe, but it keeps well; this quantity is meant for a large shrimp boil party.

Stock Island, Florida.

Spicy Orange Dipping Sauce

Chef John Smith, Hemingway's | Santa Rosa Island, Florida

Chef Smith uses this sauce for dipping his coconut shrimp, but draw on your imagination for other purposes, including a topping for broiled or fried mild-flavored fish.

Makes about 1 1/2 cups

INGREDIENTS

1 cup orange marmalade
½ teaspoon coarse-ground mustard
Juice of 1 Key lime
¼ cup finely diced pineapple
⅛ cup finely diced red bell pepper
⅛ cup finely diced red onion
1 sprig fresh cilantro (about 5 leaves),
   finely chopped

PROCESS

Combine all the ingredients in a bowl and refrigerate for 1 hour before serving.

Forces beyond Nature

The Spirit World: Of Bones, Bottles, and Bananas

One of the entertaining aspects of life in the South is the prevalence of ghost stories. Even the most conservative people I met over the course of seven years in Georgia had an encounter tale, or at least secondhand knowledge of otherworldly visitors from a cousin or neighbor. Ghost hunters frequent many southern coastal towns, especially Charleston, New Orleans, and Savannah, placing laurels of "America's Most Haunted City" on their steepled heads. One of the more unusual reports I heard came from a young woman who described how on a windless winter's evening her crystal chandelier began to shake, followed by the jiggling of certain bouncy parts of her person, while everything else remained still. That the South is fond of the liquid form of spirits perhaps comes into play, but in any event, ghosts, aliens, and a host of other presences are accepted, sometimes feared, and often welcomed by members of the communities.

There's the Ancient Mariner aspect of the good- and mostly bad-luck omens on board fishing boats, for starters. Captain Shep Owens of Stock Island,

Florida, says if he finds feathers on deck on the day he's heading out to sea, it's going to be a profitable trip. Captain Antoine Gilliard makes sure his Rockville, South Carolina-based crew never whistles on board ("you don't whistle for the wind") or sets their caps upside down ("upside-down hat, upside-down boat"). If he sees a bird with a shrimp or fish in its beak, he knows it will be a good trip. Captain William Kemp of Tybee Island, Georgia, bans bananas and peanuts on board, considered common sources of bad luck ("They're monkey food—and you don't want a monkey on your back"). The captains never head out on Fridays, and don't allow women on board.

New Orleans' voodoo history is well known, with its red brick dust lines across thresholds and pinned dolls, but the root medicine of South Carolina and Georgia's Gullah regions is equally powerful. Louisiana's voodoo was born from the marriage of African and French Catholic beliefs, where root medicine comes from African practices grafted to more austere English Methodist and Baptist traditions. On Daufuskie Island in South Carolina you'll see painted deer bones nailed onto loblolly pine trees and haint ("haunt" in Gullah) blue paint around doorways and windows to keep evil spirits out. There are also

spirit bottle trees that are meant to lure and trap unwanted presences . . . the list goes on. It's the flip side of the coin of this churchgoing region. ❧

Dijon-Mayo Dipping Sauce

Chef Joel St. John, St. John's Fire Food Truck | Houston, Texas

Chef St. John uses this dip for his Shrimp Corn Dogs (see recipe, page 59), but it's great with just about anything fried.

Makes about 1 1/2 cups

INGREDIENTS

½ cup Dijon mustard
1 cup mayonnaise
1 tablespoon fresh lemon juice
Pinch of cayenne pepper

PROCESS

Combine all the ingredients in a bowl; serve immediately.

Spicy Cream Sauce

Chef Joel St. John, St. John's Fire Food Truck | Houston, Texas

A silky, delicious sauce for dipping your shrimp into or to accompany baked mild fish like swai or tilapia.

Makes about 2 cups

INGREDIENTS

2 cups whipping cream
1 tablespoon hot sauce

PROCESS

1 Bring the cream and hot sauce to a rolling boil in a heavy pot and cook until thick, about 10 minutes. Do not let the sauce boil over.

2 Remove from the heat; serve warm.

Facing: Hobo Seafood's *Blackbeard* painted by Jimmy "Can-Do" Thompson, Swanquarter, North Carolina.

Five-Pepper Jelly

Chef Tory McPhail, Commander's Palace | New Orleans, Louisiana

Chef McPhail serves this jelly with her Shrimp and Tasso Henican (see recipe, page 74), but it would also be delicious on cornbread or as a kicky dip for grilled or fried shrimp.

Makes about 4 cups

INGREDIENTS

1½ cups light corn syrup

1¼ cups distilled white vinegar

½ teaspoon red pepper flakes

Salt and freshly ground black pepper to taste

3 large bell peppers (1 each red, yellow, and green), finely diced

4 jalapeño peppers, finely diced

PROCESS

1 Put the corn syrup, vinegar, red pepper flakes, and salt and black pepper in a small saucepan. Simmer until the mixture is thickened and has reduced by two thirds. It will get even thicker as it cools, but the peppers will thin it again when they're added.

2 Put the bell peppers in a hot, dry skillet and cook, stirring, until tender and their color is brightened, about 30 seconds. Using a slotted spoon, remove the peppers from the pan and add them to the corn syrup mixture.

3 Allow to cool before serving.

Tartar Sauce

Tartar sauce is as common as it comes for dipping fried shrimp and fish, but I've heard tell of people using it to make tuna and ham salad or to top fried green tomatoes or baked potatoes, too. I'm a citrus junky so tend to always add more lemon juice than a recipe calls for, but for this one I resist to keep the consistency creamy rather than drippy. Feel free to monkey around with the amount of diced gherkins, though, if you like your tartar sauce sweeter.

Makes about 1 cup

INGREDIENTS

½ cup mayonnaise

¼ cup sour cream

1 tablespoon sweet onion, finely grated,
    with juice

2 tablespoons finely diced gherkins or
    sweet relish

1 tablespoon capers, drained

1 tablespoon fresh lemon juice

½ teaspoon salt

⅛ teaspoon freshly ground black pepper

PROCESS

Combine all the ingredients in a bowl; cover and refrigerate for at least 1 hour before serving.

Overleaf: An abandoned tugboat along pristine Rainbow Beach on Little St. Simons Island, Georgia, gives visitors a castaway feeling.

Spiced Yogurt Dip

Nisrine Merzouki, Dinner & Dreams | www.dinnersanddreams.net

This is a perfect dip for Moroccan Baked Shrimp (see recipe, page 185) but is equally well paired with raw vegetables, falafel, or pita chips.

Makes 1 cup

INGREDIENTS

1 cup plain yogurt (or strained yogurt for a thicker consistency)

1 garlic clove, minced or pressed

½ teaspoon fresh thyme leaves or finely chopped fresh mint leaves

½ teaspoon ground cumin

½ teaspoon ground coriander

¼ teaspoon ground cinnamon

⅛ teaspoon ground cardamom

⅛ teaspoon chili powder

A pinch of cayenne pepper

Sea salt and freshly ground black pepper to taste

PROCESS

Combine all the ingredients in a bowl. Stir them well to combine the flavors.

Tomato Fondue

Chef Adam Miller, Amen Street Fish & Raw Bar | Charleston, South Carolina

I've seen versions of this recipe called tomato jam; there are lots of uses for this sauce, including as a dip for grilled or steamed shrimp, a sandwich condiment, or bruschetta sauce. I bet it's also great as is on pasta, with some spicy sausage like ground chorizo or andouille in the mix.

Makes about 2 cups

INGREDIENTS

1 (32-ounce) can diced tomatoes, drained

¼ cup red wine vinegar

1 shallot, finely minced

2 garlic cloves, finely minced

1 teaspoon freshly ground black pepper

3 tablespoons whipping cream

PROCESS

1 Puree all the ingredients in a food processer or blender until slightly chunky.

2 Bring to a simmer and cook for 10 minutes.

Ruddy turnstones, Tybee Island, Georgia.

three

Starters

In the Beginning

Shrimp are a great finger food with their convenient tails, but they perform beautifully in a wide range of appetizing starters, whether served at formal, sit-up-straight dinners or accompanying cold ones while watching the game.

Shrimping interests are advertised with this sculpture along Seawall Boulevard, Galveston Island, Texas.

Pickled Shrimp

Chef Fred Neuville, Fat Hen | Johns Island, South Carolina

Fat Hen's menu is rich with delicious concoctions, but this recipe comes from Chef Neuville's grandmother, Jewel Kizzia of Tryon, North Carolina. Make it ahead of time—it's best if it sits for a day or two.

Serves 6

INGREDIENTS

1 large onion, diced

1 stalk celery, sliced

1 medium carrot, diced

½ jalapeño pepper, seeds scraped out, sliced into thin rings

1 small bulb fennel, diced

1 tablespoon kosher salt

Grated zest and juice of 1 large lemon

Grated zest and juice of 1 orange

5 cloves garlic, peeled

1 bay leaf

1 tablespoon whole black peppercorns

1 teaspoon ground coriander

1 teaspoon mustard seeds

½ cup sugar

1 cup cider vinegar

1 cup tarragon vinegar

4 ounces French green beans, cut into ½-inch pieces

1 pound (21- to 25-count) shrimp, peeled and deveined

Grilled bread

A few small heirloom tomatoes, sliced

1 cucumber, sliced

Rémoulade (see recipe, page 31)

PROCESS

1 Put everything in a pot except the shrimp, bread, tomatoes, cucumbers, and rémoulade. Bring to a boil and cook for 3 minutes.

2 Put the shrimp in a heatproof container. Pour the boiling liquid over the shrimp and stir well.

3 Transfer to a sealed plastic or glass container. Let sit overnight (or longer), shaking it occasionally to make sure the flavors distribute.

4 Serve with grilled bread, tomatoes, cucumbers, and rémoulade.

Grilled Shrimp

Jill Ferree | Tybee Island, Georgia

Mrs. Ferree's son, Chef Kurtis Schumm of the Tybee Island Social Club, likes these shrimp on po'boys; in grilled corn tortilla tacos with red onion, cilantro, and queso fresco; over grits or rice; or served chilled in a pasta salad. But they're great just as peel-and-eat delicacies, too. This is Chef Schumm's slightly altered version of his mom's recipe.

Serves 8

INGREDIENTS

½ cup apple cider vinegar

1 tablespoon cayenne pepper

½ cup olive oil

¾ cup honey

1 tablespoon salt

½ tablespoon cracked black pepper

¼ teaspoon ground ginger

1 tablespoon marjoram powder

1 teaspoon ground cardamom

1 teaspoon ground allspice

1 teaspoon garlic powder

1 teaspoon onion powder

2 pounds deveined shrimp, shells on

PROCESS

1 Whisk all ingredients except the shrimp together in a large bowl; add the shrimp and toss to coat well. Cover and refrigerate overnight (or transfer to sealed bags and refrigerate, shaking bag a few times).

2 Build a charcoal fire; grill the shrimp for 1½ minutes on each side, then let them rest on the platter for a few minutes before serving.

Facing: Southern fly repellant: water in a sandwich bag, hung at outside eateries and on porches across the southern states. Snopes and *MythBusters* have each tackled disproving its effectiveness, which believers attribute to the refracted light somehow confusing flies' eyes; the former came up with an "inconclusive" report, while the latter deemed the myth "busted."

Overleaf: Tybee Island Hives beekeeper Dave Strickland checks on his troops, Tybee Island, Georgia. Photo by Jay Fleming.

Wild Truffled Shrimp

Chef Sibrand Johan Jurriaans, Prima Bistro | Langley, Washington
(Whidbey Island)

The flavors in this elegant, original dish are nothing short of addictive; the sauce is like a divine shallot jam. While Chef Jurriaans is based in Washington, he uses Gulf shrimp for this recipe.

Serves 4

INGREDIENTS

4 tablespoons canola oil

1 pound shrimp (16- to 20-count), peeled and deveined

1 cup Marcona almonds

¼ cup chopped shallots

¾ cup good-quality honey

½ teaspoon salt, or to taste

½ teaspoon freshly ground black pepper, or to taste

¼ cup fresh fines herbs (mixture of chopped parsley, tarragon, chives, and fennel fronds)

4 teaspoons white truffle oil

Sea salt

PROCESS

1 Coat a sauté pan with the canola oil and heat until smoking; sear the shrimp quickly on both sides, then remove from pan.

2 Add the almonds and shallots and sauté until the shallots are soft, about 5 minutes.

3 Add the honey and seared shrimp. Simmer until the shrimp are cooked through, just after they turn orange-pink all the way through, about 3 minutes.

4 Season with salt and pepper to taste and add in herbs.

5 Divide among four serving bowls; drizzle with truffle oil and sprinkle with sea salt and serve.

Shrimp Empanadas
with Pineapple Salsa

Chef Russell Midgett, Rusty's Surf & Turf | Hatteras, North Carolina

When I first met Rusty, he was a surfing, motorcycle-riding teenager who took the time to show me around Hatteras as only someone whose family has lived there for centuries can. Decades later, he's still surfing—but has leveraged a Culinary Institute diploma and experience in some of Philadelphia's finest restaurants into his own place at home.

Makes 40 empanadas

INGREDIENTS

2 cups drained canned crushed pineapple (or mango, or a mixture of the two)

¼ small red onion, diced

3 tablespoons chopped fresh cilantro

Juice of ½ lime

Pinch of salt

1½ pounds shrimp, peeled, deveined, and chopped

2 packets of Goya Sazón seasoning

2 tablespoons extra-virgin olive oil

½ red bell pepper, diced

½ green bell pepper, diced

½ bunch scallions, sliced

½ tablespoon minced garlic

½ cup panko bread crumbs

40 empanada tortillas (available in most larger grocery stores)

Egg wash (1 egg beaten with ¼ cup milk)

Vegetable shortening for frying

PROCESS

1 Combine the pineapple, red onion, cilantro, lime juice, and salt in a bowl; let rest for 1 hour.

2 Sauté the shrimp with 1 packet of the Goya Sazón and half of the oil in a large pan until cooked through. Transfer to a shallow pan and let cool; do not drain.

3 Sauté the bell peppers, scallions, and garlic with the remaining Goya Sazón packet in the remaining oil until softened. Transfer to a shallow pan and let cool; do not drain.

4 When cool, combine the shrimp and the bell pepper mixture with the bread crumbs. Cover and let the mixture rest in the refrigerator for at least 1 hour to allow the flavors to marry and the bread crumbs to absorb the extra liquid. (This can be done 1 day in advance.)

5 Place 4 tablespoons of the shrimp mixture in the center of an empanada tortilla, moisten the rim of the tortilla with egg wash, and fold into a half-moon. Carefully squeeze out excess air and crimp the edges with a fork. This can be done a few hours in advance; refrigerate the empanadas until you're ready to fry them.

6 Fry in batches, turning as the shrimp become golden, in 350°F vegetable shortening, 3 to 5 minutes.

7 Serve with the pineapple salsa.

Dilly Fried Shrimp

Chef Donna Leibbert | Galveston, Texas

In addition to contributing her culinary skills to the island, Chef Leibbert aided Galveston through a campaign to bring in carvers to reimagine the remains of live oak trees left behind when Hurricane Ike's toxic waters receded. See page 108 for the story.

Serves 4 (or more as a pass-around)

INGREDIENTS

⅔ cup plus ½ cup finely chopped dill pickles

½ cup sour cream

¼ cup mayonnaise

2 eggs, beaten

½ cup dill pickle juice

½ teaspoon salt

½ teaspoon freshly ground black pepper

1 pound large shrimp, shelled and deveined

½ cup panko bread crumbs

½ teaspoon dried dill weed

1½ cups all-purpose flour

Vegetable oil for deep frying

PROCESS

1 Make the sauce the morning of your meal (or the day before) by whisking the ⅔ cup pickles, the sour cream, and mayonnaise together in a bowl. Refrigerate in a sealed container.

2 Combine the eggs, ½ cup pickles, the pickle juice, salt, and pepper, then add the shrimp. Marinate in a sealed bag or covered bowl in the refrigerator for about 3 hours.

3 Combine the bread crumbs, dill, and flour.

4 Drain the shrimp and dredge them in the breadcrumb-flour mixture.

5 Fry at 375°F for 2 to 4 minutes, until golden brown. Serve with the sauce.

Shrimp Corn Dogs

Chef Joel St. John, St. John's Fire Food Truck | Houston, Texas

This new twist on an old favorite was featured on the show *Eat Street*.

Serves 4

INGREDIENTS

2 cups all-purpose flour

½ cup cornstarch

2 large eggs

2 cups buttermilk

2½ cups cornmeal

1 teaspoon baking powder

1 teaspoon baking soda

¼ cup chopped fresh parsley

1 tablespoon Creole seasoning

2 tablespoons vegetable oil, plus more
   for deep frying

16 extra-large shrimp, tails on, peeled and
   deveined

Dijon-Mayo Dipping Sauce (see recipe,
   page 38)

PROCESS

1 Whisk 1 cup of the flour and the cornstarch together in shallow bowl; set aside.

2 To make the batter, in a separate bowl whisk the eggs and buttermilk together; add the remaining 1 cup flour, the cornmeal, baking powder, baking soda, parsley, Creole seasoning, and 2 tablespoons oil.

3 Using sixteen 6-inch skewers, thread each shrimp onto a skewer through the tail toward the head, dredge in the flour-cornstarch mixture, then dip in the batter, rubbing off the excess.

4 Hold the shrimp by the stick and submerge in 350°F oil, carefully holding the stick until the batter starts to cook. Let go and fry for 4 minutes, until golden.

5 Serve with Dijon-Mayo Dipping Sauce.

Toasted Coriander Shrimp
with Olives and Feta on Hummus

Chef John Skaggs, The Heirloom Cafe | Columbus, Ohio

I play a little search engine game where I plug in the word "shrimp" and then every spice, condiment, and other flavor I can think of, just to see if anyone has tried to join them into a recipe. Some are obvious: Bacon and lemon are pretty regular partners to shrimp. Others are less so (say, eggplant), but I've never failed to find a recipe online this way. I love coriander, so this was one of the combinations I looked at. I found Chef Skaggs's toasted coriander seed vinaigrette in a more general search of the spice; his dressing sounded like a divine base for a shrimp recipe. And so it now is, thanks to Chef's good-natured acceptance of my request to develop a shrimp recipe that incorporates it. He may be in Ohio, but he wrote this haiku—and poetry inspired by a shrimp recipe feels like the South to me!

Smell coriander,
Toasting sweet hot crackling pop!
Closed eyes take a bite.

Serves 4

PITA CHIPS INGREDIENTS

4 pitas
Olive oil
Ground coriander
Salt and freshly ground black pepper

HUMMUS INGREDIENTS

3 cups cooked, rinsed, and drained
    garbanzo beans
2 tablespoons fresh lemon juice
1 teaspoon salt
2 tablespoons tahini
2 cloves roasted garlic, mashed (about 2
    teaspoons)

SHRIMP INGREDIENTS

1 tablespoon coriander seeds

1½ teaspoons salt

½ teaspoon whole black peppercorns

5 tablespoons extra-virgin olive oil

¼ cup minced shallot

1 small clove garlic, minced

1 pound peeled and deveined extra-large or colossal shrimp

3 tablespoons white balsamic vinegar

Grated zest and juice of ¼ lemon

¼ cup cubed feta cheese

¼ cup pitted Kalamata olives

PITA CHIPS PROCESS

1 Split and brush the pitas with a little oil and sprinkle with coriander and salt and pepper.

2 Cut each half in half again, then cut into triangles.

3 Cook in a single layer on a baking sheet at 400°F for 5 minutes.

HUMMUS PROCESS

Puree all the ingredients in a food processor, gradually adding 2 to 4 tablespoons water, until a smooth paste forms.

SHRIMP PROCESS

1 Stir the coriander seeds in a small dry skillet over medium heat until fragrant, about 4 minutes.

2 Let cool, then coarsely grind with the salt and pepper in a mortar and pestle or spice mill.

3 Heat 2 tablespoons of the oil in the same skillet over medium heat. Add the shallots and garlic; sauté until just soft, about 1 minute.

4 Increase the heat to high. Sprinkle the shrimp with the coriander mixture. Add the shrimp to the skillet and sauté until the shrimp are opaque, about 3 minutes. Reduce the heat to low.

5 Add the vinegar and lemon zest and juice, and deglaze the pan. Gradually stir in the 3 remaining tablespoons of oil.

6 Spoon the hummus onto individual plates and top with the shrimp, cheese, and olives. Serve with the pita chips.

Shrimp Stack

Chef Chris Rainosek, The Wash House | Fairhope, Alabama

It's a magical place, the Alabama coast—providing scenes and conversations that seem drawn more from a dream or magical novel than reality; Chef Rainosek adds to the experience with his original and bountiful menu. The Wash House is one of those restaurants I'll drive well out of my way to visit.

Serves 4

INGREDIENTS

2 pounds large ripe tomatoes

1 yellow onion, sliced

6 cloves garlic, smashed

¼ cup olive oil

2 teaspoons salt, plus more to taste

1 teaspoon freshly ground black pepper,
   plus more to taste

1 tablespoon dried oregano

1 tablespoon chopped fresh parsley

1 teaspoon red pepper flakes

2 tablespoons red wine vinegar

About 2 cups whipping cream

8 (¼-inch-thick) slices green tomato

2 cups buttermilk

Canola oil for frying

2 cups all-purpose flour

2 cups yellow cornmeal

1 ball fresh buffalo mozzarella cheese,
   sliced

8 extra-large deveined shrimp, cooked,
   shells removed, tails on

PROCESS

1 Preheat the oven to 300°F. Cut the red tomatoes into large pieces, then toss with the onion, garlic, olive oil, salt, and black pepper. Place on a baking sheet and roast for 2 hours.

2 Remove from the oven and puree in a food processor or blender with the oregano, parsley, red pepper flakes, and vinegar. Taste the tomato sauce and add salt and pepper if needed.

3 Measure the tomato sauce; it should be about 4 cups. Add to a pan with the 2 cups cream (you want a 2 to 1 ratio of sauce to cream). Simmer the mixture for 15 minutes over low heat. Set aside.

4 Soak the green tomatoes in the buttermilk.

5 Fill a heavy pot with 1 inch of canola oil. Heat the oil to 350 to 375°F.

6 Mix together the flour and cornmeal in a bowl; season with salt and pepper.

7 Remove the green tomatoes from the buttermilk and shake off any excess liquid. Toss in the cornmeal mixture and gently place in the hot oil, working in batches. Fry until golden brown, 3 to 5 minutes total, until golden. Remove to paper towels to soak up excess oil.

8 To build the stacks, place one slice of the cheese between two warm fried green tomatoes. Place the stack on a plate, top with some tomato cream sauce, and place one shrimp on either side of the stack. Serve immediately.

Sometimes the Shrimp Come to You

The Maritime Mystery of Mobile Bay's Jubilee Events

On steamy summer nights along Mobile Bay's coast, when fresh water swirls with the salty Gulf of Mexico and winds press down just so, sea creatures come ashore in droves of their own volition: slithering eels, flapping flounder, crawling shrimp, and scrambling crabs. So many beach themselves that folks spread the word to their sleeping neighbors, ringing bells along the waterfront back in the day, and through phone calls in this more recent era. They come armed with buckets, nets, bushel baskets, and gigs to haul in the free catch that's known as a jubilee. It happens every summer, sometimes more than once, usually in August just before dawn—but all of the timing and the right conditions can be present without the same effect. This fable-worthy exodus has been scarcely recorded elsewhere in the world, but it's only here along a short stretch of Alabama's eastern coast between Daphne and Point Clear that it's a reliable annual ritual.

Part of the magic is that even in this advanced technological age, the

occurrence remains unpredictable. Texas Sea Grant agent Tony Reisinger, whose mother hailed from Mobile, helps to explain by referencing Edwin May's 1930s studies—but also admits no one really knows for sure how jubilees come to be. "Estuaries have a dense saltwater wedge that slips like a long tongue reaching from the ocean's side underneath the less dense, fresher bay water. Jubilees can occur when that bottom water, oxygen deprived from decaying organic matter, is pushed onto the shallow eastern shelf of the bay. The incoming tide sometimes coaxes the low-oxygen—hypoxic—water toward the shallows, driving marine life to seek refuge along the eastern shoreline, where in early morning, already low levels of oxygen are being consumed, not produced, by algae in the water. This doesn't explain everything, because the result is not always a jubilee. It could be that the easterly wind that's usually present is another factor in the equation, and that adds to the enigma. Ultimately, I've always thought of jubilee as one of the mysteries of life I simply have to accept without question, having those bay waters in my veins."

With a home smack on the water, Point Clear resident Ralph Reynolds has experienced a number of jubilees.

He describes the atmosphere preceding the event as dead still and humid. One recent summer morning, he was heading out to the Gulf around 6:30 a.m. when he heard a commotion and saw gulls and herons swooping down and crowding his pier. From his porch, he could make out some boats and people with flounder gigs and nets. Walking down to the beach, he saw the shrimp, crabs, and flounder piling up, and soon learned how determined the creatures were: "A gull dropped an eel on my head; I threw it back in the water, only to see it shimmy right back onto shore." He scooped up all the shrimp he could for an impromptu feast that night.

Sometimes the jubilee forces more of one kind of creature than another out of Mobile Bay; on one occasion, Ralph said, the sand was so filled with eels buried up to their necks, all of them gasping for air, that it was hard to walk without stepping on one. "It was like the sand had sprouted Medusa heads." ❧

An old-school Texas dance hall, Corpus Christi, Texas.

Acapulco Bar-B-Que Shrimp

Susie Rucker | Corpus Christi, Texas

The first thing to know about southern barbecued shrimp is that no barbecue sauce is used! This recipe was inspired by a dish the Ruckers enjoyed in Mexico; Susie reinvented the sauce from her tastebuds' memory.

Serves 4 to 6

INGREDIENTS

1 cup mayonnaise

¼ cup prepared chili sauce

1 tablespoon fresh lemon juice

1 tablespoon Worcestershire sauce

Dash of hot sauce

Pinch of salt

2 pounds jumbo shrimp

½ cup (1 stick) butter, melted

PROCESS

1 Combine the first 6 ingredients together in a bowl and stir until smooth; set aside.

2 Pull the legs (and heads, if still on) from the shrimp; wash them and slit them along the back to the tail, leaving the shells on. Devein and pat them dry.

3 Prepare an even but not blazing bed of coals in an outdoor grill.

4 Brush the shrimp with melted butter and carefully lay them on a well-scrubbed grill grate with their tails sticking up.

5 Cover and cook until the shrimp are pink, 3 minutes or so.

6 Remove the shrimp from the grill and arrange them on a platter.

7 Serve the sauce in ramekins or small bowls for dipping. Guests will peel their shrimp, so provide bowls for the shells.

Tip: When serving shrimp as a peel-and-eat dish, provide washcloths dampened with lemon water for your guests in addition to lots of napkins.

Shrimp Okonomiyaki with Fish Sauce Aioli and Nori Toasted Peanuts

Chef Stephen Phelps, Indigenous | Sarasota, Florida

Okonomiyaki is a griddled Japanese savory pancake made from a variety of ingredients. Chef Phelps, a James Beard Award semifinalist, takes his inspiration from versions served by street vendors to showcase the shrimp coming from his Gulf Coast front yard.

Serves 4 to 6

FISH SAUCE AIOLI INGREDIENTS

2 cups fish sauce

Juice of 2 limes

½ cup sugar

1 clove garlic, minced

1 tablespoon minced fresh cilantro

1 small red chile, thinly sliced

2 teaspoons grated fresh ginger

1½ cups mayonnaise

NORI TOASTED PEANUTS INGREDIENTS

1 cup roasted peanuts (with salt is best)

1 sheet nori (dried seaweed)

1 teaspoon curry powder

1 tablespoon vegetable oil

CUCUMBER INGREDIENTS

1 large European cucumber, seeded and diced

¼ cup fresh basil

OKONOMYAKI INGREDIENTS

4 large eggs

1 small head green or red cabbage, finely shredded

1 carrot, grated

1 cup julienned kale

½ cup rice flour

3 tablespoons vegetable oil

Salt and freshly ground black pepper

SHRIMP INGREDIENTS

2 tablespoons oil

1 pound shrimp, peeled and deveined

FISH SAUCE AIOLI PROCESS

Whisk all the ingredients together with 1 cup water in a mixing bowl until smooth. Cover and refrigerate until needed.

NORI TOASTED PEANUTS PROCESS

1 Preheat the oven to 400°F. Place the peanuts, nori, and curry powder in a food processor and pulse until very broken up, but do not overprocess or it will turn to peanut butter.

2 Toss with the oil and spread out on a baking sheet. Toast in the oven for 8 to 10 minutes, until the peanuts are golden. Remove from the oven and let cool.

CUCUMBERS PROCESS

Toss the cucumbers in a bowl with the basil; set aside.

OKONOMIYAKI PROCESS

1 For the pancake: Beat the eggs together in a large mixing bowl. Add the cabbage, carrot, and kale. Toss together with the rice flour.

2 Heat the oil in a large skillet. Slowly add the cabbage mixture until a thick pielike pancake shape is made. Cook on both sides until crisp, remove to paper towels, and season with salt and pepper.

SHRIMP PROCESS

1 Heat the oil in a medium skillet, add the shrimp, and sauté until just cooked through, about 3 minutes.

2 Reheat the cabbage pancake in the oven on a baking sheet for about 5 minutes.

3 Remove the pancake from the oven and place it on a platter. Top with the shrimp, then the cucumber mixture. Drizzle with the aioli and sprinkle with a generous amount of the peanuts. Serve as desired; sliced like a pizza is best.

Overleaf: Bait for sale at Bradenton Beach's pier, Anna Maria Island, Florida.

Shrimp Pâté

Mrs. A. C. Hartridge | St. Simons Island, Georgia
From the Cassina Garden Club's 1937 edition of *Coastal Cookery*

Shrimp pâté is a fabulous Jazz Age sort of recipe that you'd imagine servants presenting on silver platters or beautiful china. Use cookie cutters to make pâté shapes to put on top of cucumber slices or crackers, garnished with dill or pimento. The pâté can also be used as filler for tea sandwiches or a layer of an interesting seafood Napoleon.

Serves 16 or more

INGREDIENTS

1½ pounds shrimp, steamed in seafood boil spice, shelled, and deveined

½ cup (1 stick) butter, softened, plus 2 tablespoons

1 teaspoon salt

1½ teaspoons Worcestershire sauce

Pinch of cayenne pepper

Pinch of freshly ground black pepper

Toasted bread crumbs

PROCESS

1 Puree the shrimp in a food processor until a smooth paste forms.

2 Mix in the ½ cup of softened butter and the seasonings and blend to a butterlike consistency.

3 Press into a loaf pan and cover with toasted bread crumbs. Dot with the remaining 2 tablespoons butter.

4 Bake at 450°F for 10 to 15 minutes, until the bread crumb topping is golden brown.

5 Let cool completely, then invert the pan and remove the pâté to a platter; chill, covered, for 2 hours or so.

6 Cut into ¼- to ½-inch slices.

Lightkeeper's residence reflection, St. Simons Island, Georgia.

Shrimp and Tasso Henican

Chef Tory McPhail, Commander's Palace | New Orleans, Louisiana

This is one of the most popular dishes at Commander's Palace, for good reason. The spicy and the sweet, the mix of textures, the pretty colors . . . it wins on every level.

Serves 8

INGREDIENTS

24 jumbo shrimp, peeled and deveined

2 ounces tasso ham (see note), cut into 24 (1-inch) strips

½ cup all-purpose flour

Creole seasoning

½ cup vegetable oil

¾ cup Hot Sauce Beurre Blanc (see recipe, page 33)

¾ cup Five-Pepper Jelly (see recipe, page 40)

12 pickled okra pods, cut in half top to bottom

PROCESS

1 Cut a ¼-inch-deep incision down the back of each shrimp where it has been deveined, and place a ham strip in each incision. Secure with a toothpick lengthwise.

2 Combine the flour with Creole seasoning to taste and lightly dredge each shrimp in the mixture.

3 Heat the oil in a large skillet over medium heat and fry the shrimp in the hot oil for about 30 seconds on each side, until the shrimp are firm, with a red-brown color. Remove the shrimp from the oil and drain briefly on a paper towel.

4 Toss the shrimp with the beurre blanc in a bowl to coat thoroughly, then remove the toothpicks.

5 Place a portion of the jelly on each of eight appetizer plates, and arrange 3 shrimp on each plate, alternating with 3 pieces of pickled okra.

Note: Tasso is a seasoned ham widely used in New Orleans but hard to find elsewhere. You could order it by mail, or substitute cured or smoked regular ham. My dad used to use regular ham tossed with cayenne pepper and paprika in a pinch.

Cajun Egg Rolls

Chef Joel St. John, St. John's Fire Food Truck | Houston, Texas

Chef St. John's kicky dishes have won awards and been featured on the Food Network and Cooking Channel. His is one of the top food trucks in Houston; people stand in line for this killer gourmet egg roll.

Makes 10 large or 30 small egg rolls

INGREDIENTS

1 small yellow onion, diced

1 red bell pepper, diced

1 hot chile (Anaheim, poblano, jalapeño, etc.), diced

2 stalks celery, diced

Vegetable oil

8 ounces andouille sausage, finely diced

8 ounces small shrimp, peeled and deveined

8 ounces crawfish tails

Cajun seasoning to taste (Chef St. John has his own J.S.J. Louisiana Spark, but use what you can find)

4 ounces spinach (½ bag), chopped

¾ cup guava jelly

¼ cup Creole mustard

2 cups whipping cream

3 teaspoons hot sauce

Egg roll or wonton wrappers

PROCESS

1 Sauté the onion, bell pepper, chile, and celery in 1 tablespoon oil in a skillet over medium-high heat for 3 minutes. Add the sausage, shrimp, crawfish tails, and Creole seasoning. Cook until the shrimp turn pink, about 3 minutes. Remove from the heat.

2 Add the spinach to the skillet and stir well. Drain off all the excess liquid. Let the filling cool completely.

3 Whisk the jelly and mustard together in a bowl. Set aside.

4 In a heavy saucepan, boil the cream and hot sauce until thick and reduced, about 10 minutes. Do not let the sauce boil over. Set aside.

5 Following the package directions, roll the shrimp filling into the egg roll wrappers. Deep fry in 350°F oil until golden brown. Serve with the guava mustard and spicy cream sauces on the side.

Shrimp Ceviche

Chef Shannon Spillers | Harlingen, Texas

Don't fret—the acid from the limes "cooks" the shrimp. There's no need to heat this up.

Serves 8 to 10

INGREDIENTS

5 large Roma tomatoes, finely diced

1 white onion, finely diced

½ bunch fresh cilantro, finely chopped

5 large jalapeños, membranes and seeds
   removed, minced

4 cups Gulf shrimp (21- to 25-count),
   peeled, deveined, and diced

Grated zest of 1 lime

1 cup fresh lime juice

2 teaspoons sea salt

Saltine crackers

PROCESS

Mix all the ingredients except the crackers together thoroughly; cover and refrigerate for 30 to 45 minutes, turning occasionally until the shrimp become opaque. Serve with crackers.

Gambas al Ajillo (Garlic Shrimp)

Chef Colette Nelson, Ludvig's Bistro | Sitka, Alaska
(Baranof Island)

Ludvig's Bistro is Sitka's fine dining center. Chef Nelson serves the onslaught of guests brought to the harbor by cruise ships and resident islanders with equal aplomb, marrying local seafood, sea salt, and vegetables from the brief Alaskan summer to Mediterranean culinary traditions. For this recipe she uses Alaska's spot prawns, available for only the blink of an eye, but Gulf or Atlantic shrimp will work just fine.

Serves 4

INGREDIENTS

½ cup extra-virgin olive oil

1 tablespoon chopped garlic

1 teaspoon smoked paprika

1 teaspoon red pepper flakes

1 pound medium shrimp, shelled and
   deveined

¼ cup dry sherry

Juice of 1 lemon

Salt and freshly ground black pepper
   to taste

3 teaspoons chopped fresh parsley

Grilled bread

PROCESS

1 Warm the oil in a sauté pan over medium heat. Add the garlic, smoked paprika, and red pepper flakes and cook, stirring, until the garlic is browned, about 2 minutes.

2 Add the shrimp, sherry, and lemon juice and sauté until the shrimp are just pink, 2 to 3 minutes.

3 Season with salt and black pepper, and toss with the parsley.

4 Arrange the shrimp on a serving plate; drizzle the sauce from the pan over the shrimp. Serve with grilled bread.

Texas Shrimp Dip

Chef Kent Rathbun, Jasper's | Plano, Austin, and Houston, Texas

This rich and flavorful dip can be served bubbling hot or at room temperature, for football games or holiday parties.

Serves 4 to 6

INGREDIENTS

2 tablespoons olive oil

2 tablespoons minced garlic

½ cup sour cream

¼ cup feta cheese, crumbled

1 pound (2 packages) cream cheese, softened

¼ cup boursin cheese, crumbled

¼ cup Parmesan cheese, grated

1 teaspoon green hot sauce

1 tablespoon Worcestershire sauce

2 tablespoons chopped fresh basil leaves

2 tablespoons minced fresh chives

1 tablespoon salt

1 tablespoon cracked pepper

Juice of 2 lemons

1 pound steamed shrimp, coarsely chopped in a food processor

½ cup bread crumbs

PROCESS

1 Preheat the oven to 350°F.

2 In a large sauté pan, heat the oil over medium heat and add the garlic; cook until softened. Remove from the heat.

3 In a food processor, combine the garlic and oil, sour cream, feta, cream cheese, Boursin, and Parmesan; puree until smooth.

4 Transfer to a bowl and stir in the hot sauce, Worcestershire sauce, basil, chives, salt, pepper, and lemon juice.

5 Gently fold in the shrimp.

6 Spread in a casserole dish and top with a thin layer of bread crumbs; cover with foil.

7 Bake for 15 minutes, then uncover and bake for 15 minutes longer, or until golden brown on top. Serve hot.

Linda's Shrimp Dip

Chef Karey Lynn Butterworth, Glow | Rockport, Texas

This recipe comes courtesy of Chef Butterworth's mother, who served it for special occasions.

Serves 12

INGREDIENTS

Seasoning for boiled shrimp (bay leaf, Tabasco sauce, black peppercorns, lemon slices)

8 ounces deveined medium to large shrimp, shells on

8 ounces (1 package) cream cheese, softened

½ cup mayonnaise

Juice of ½ lemon

2 teaspoons Worcestershire sauce

3 tablespoons chopped scallion

2 teaspoons chopped fresh parsley

2 teaspoons garlic powder

Sea salt and cracked pepper to taste

Vegetable crudités, crackers, or sliced baguettes

PROCESS

1 Bring 6 cups water to boil in a pot. Add the seasoning mixture and the shrimp. Boil until the shrimp are cooked through, about 3 minutes.

2 Remove the shrimp from the water and let cool. Peel and finely chop the shrimp, then set aside.

3 In a large bowl, mix together the cream cheese, mayonnaise, lemon juice, Worcestershire sauce, scallion, parsley, and garlic powder. Gently fold in the chopped shrimp. Season to taste with salt and pepper.

4 Cover and refrigerate for at least 1 hour. Serve with vegetable crudités, crackers, or sliced baguettes.

5 The dip can be served hot as well; place the dip in a 2-quart baking dish and bake at 350°F for 30 minutes, or until bubbly.

Overleaf: A heron takes shelter from an incoming storm, Rockport, Texas.

True Blue

Captain Charlie Livingston, the *Babe*, Aransas Pass, Texas, and Fort Myers, Florida

You might take one look at the guy wandering around the Erickson & Jensen dock with rough bare feet sporting a soiled, ragged T-shirt and long, wild hair pulled back from his weathered face and wonder what the cat dragged in. You might struggle to understand his accent. Your gut instinct might even scoot you across the street to avoid him. But if you judged this particular book by his frayed, stained cover and use of language, you'd miss meeting one of the most successful shrimp trawler captains in the Gulf of Mexico, and a big-hearted hero to boot. Charlie Livingston is the gen-u-ine, salty article.

I was introduced to Charlie by one of the Aransas Pass fleet owners, Grant Erickson. Charlie had just filled the hold of the *Babe* with thirty thousand pounds of shrimp during a twenty-four-day trip out at sea (which explains the state of him—three weeks on an old trawler with two other guys—his wife, Judy, says she has to throw his "ripped up, ripped off" clothes away when he isn't looking). That's a tractor trailer's load of shrimp, in case you're wondering, and at that day's price per pound, a haul worth about $200,000 at market.

The shrimp tattoos across Charlie's shoulders are a testament to his pride, dedication to his work, and deep roots in the coastal life. His vision for the full-back inked tableaux includes Poseidon with a trident in his raised arm ready to "gig" the shrimp. Charlie as a Gulf Coast god isn't that much of a stretch, from the curly hair and beard to the role as protector. He learned to swim at five when his daddy tossed him overboard—with a rope—and has been in and on the water ever since. He's the kind of sailor who jumps on another captain's burning boat when everyone else is jumping off, with his head wrapped in a wet towel to breathe while he sees how he can put out the fire below and save the vessel.

Charlie's worked in the business for more than three decades and is respected as one of those captains who instinctively knows where the shrimp are beyond the previous years' reports and equipment that guides the

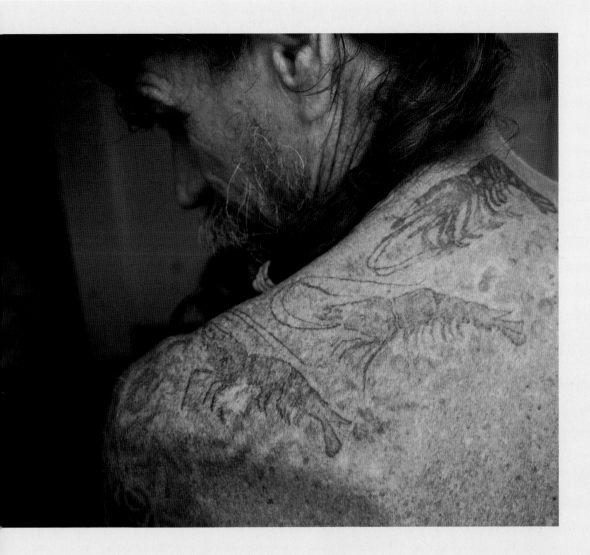

competition. As Judy says, "He'll go where most people won't—he'll fight trash on the ocean floor in the shipping lanes, risking tearing up his nets, because the shrimp are all tucked up underneath all over the place in there. He'll stay up for twelve hours fixing the nets to start again, and whatever trash he brings up from the water, he recycles when he gets back to shore." Charlie's worked for Erickson & Jensen for so long, so loyally and so well, that he's become a member of the family. He's as true blue as the ink on his skin. ❧

Campechana

Chef Antonio Galan, Galvez Bar & Grill | Galveston, Texas

Versions of this Mexican seafood cocktail are served all along the Gulf Coast; Chef Galan's stands out as the most flavorful of the many I've so valiantly sampled, in one of the most beautiful environments—the historic Hotel Galvez, the only waterfront hotel of its caliber in Texas.

Serves 4, with salsa left over

INGREDIENTS

2 cups ketchup

2 cups chili sauce

2 cups tomato-clam cocktail

½ cup fresh lime juice

1 cup green olives, minced

½ bunch fresh parsley, chopped

1 jalapeño pepper, membranes and seeds
   removed, minced

2 poblano peppers, roasted, peeled,
   seeded, and diced

2 tablespoons minced garlic

Hot sauce to taste

¾ cup olive oil

2 avocados, diced

¼ cup pico de gallo

8 ounces small steamed shrimp, shelled
   (set 4 shrimp aside for garnish)

8 ounces lump crabmeat

1 scallion, greens only, sliced,

Tortilla chips

PROCESS

1 Combine the ketchup, chili sauce, tomato-clam cocktail, lime juice, olives, parsley, jalapeño, poblano, garlic, and hot sauce in a large bowl. Slowly incorporate oil into the mixture; set aside 1 cup of this salsa, and refrigerate the rest in a sealed container for future use.

2 Mix the 1 cup salsa, the avocados, pico de gallo, shrimp, and crabmeat together.

3 Serve in footed clear glass bowls or glasses; garnish each with a single shrimp and some scallion. Place the glasses on paper napkins on small plates and spread tortilla chips around. Serve immediately.

Parmesan Peppercorn Shrimp Dip

Jane LaRoche | Rockville, South Carolina
(Wadmalaw Island)

Here's an easy appetizer, especially if you have some leftover shrimp from the night before. It's great with corn chips and beer.

Serves 6 to 8

INGREDIENTS

1 pound cooked and peeled shrimp

3 tablespoons sour cream

2 tablespoons Parmesan peppercorn salad dressing (or more, if desired)

¼ yellow onion, peeled and cut into two pieces

PROCESS

1 Pulse the cooked shrimp in a food processor or blender.

2 Remove to a bowl and mix in the sour cream and salad dressing.

3 Submerge the two onion pieces in the dip.

4 Cover and chill the dip for 1 hour; remove and discard the onion pieces and stir well before serving.

Shrimp Puppies

Annette Reddell Hegen, from *Hooked on Seafood*
for Texas A&M's Sea Grant Program

No southern cookbook would be complete without at least one hush puppy recipe; here's one that incorporates shrimp for a little more substance.

Makes 60 puppies

INGREDIENTS

2 cups cooked, peeled, and coarsely chopped shrimp

2 (6-ounce) packages of jalapeño cornbread mix

1 (17-ounce) can of creamed corn

¼ cup finely chopped scallions, including tops

1 jalapeño pepper, minced (optional)

Vegetable oil for deep frying

PROCESS

1 Coarsely chop the shrimp in a blender or food processor until it has a crumbled texture.

2 Combine the cornbread mix, creamed corn, scallions, and jalapeño (if desired) in a bowl; add the shrimp and mix well.

3 In a heavy pot, heat 2 inches of oil to 365°F.

4 Drop the shrimp mixture by heaping teaspoonfuls into the hot oil; do not crowd them in the pot. Fry until golden brown and floating on the surface of the oil.

5 Drain on paper towels or paper grocery bags and serve hot.

Note: Any of the dips in chapter 2 would be great with these, including Tartar Sauce (page 41) and Dijon-Mayo Dipping Sauce (page 38).

Cocoa plays first mate by checking the ropes aboard the *Gray Ghost* in Engelhard, North Carolina.

Shrimp and Dill Pesto Pockets

These tasty and pretty appetizers are a perfect choice for a cocktail party.

Makes 24 pockets

INGREDIENTS

24 wonton wrappers

3 tablespoons butter, softened

2 tablespoons olive oil

1 large yellow or white onion, diced

2 teaspoons minced garlic

Cayenne pepper

1 (14-ounce) can low-salt diced tomatoes, drained

1 pound medium shrimp, peeled and deveined

Dill pesto (see recipe, page 164)

¼ cup crumbled feta cheese

PROCESS

1 Preheat the oven to 350°F.

2 Lightly coat two mini-muffin tins with nonstick cooking spray.

3 Brush one side of each wonton wrapper with butter; press into a muffin tin hole, butter side up.

4 Bake the wonton shells for 7 to 8 minutes, until the edges turn a light golden brown. Set aside, leaving the oven on.

5 In a sauté pan, cook the the onion in the oil over medium-high heat until just golden, about 5 minutes; add the garlic and a couple dashes of cayenne pepper.

6 Add the tomatoes and simmer for 5 minutes.

7 Add the shrimp and cook until they turn opaque or orange-pink. Set aside to cool.

8 Coarsely chop the shrimp mixture in a blender or food processor.

9 Fill each wonton shell with 1 tablespoon of the shrimp mixture; top with ¼ teaspoon or so of the dill pesto and sprinkle with cheese.

10 Bake for 1 minute more. Serve warm.

Dappled sunlight through double screening (intended to deter ambitious raccoons) casts a moiré pattern on conch shells found in the waters of Cook Island, Florida—part of the Keys archipelago.

Blackened Shrimp
with Black-Eyed Pea Vinaigrette

Chef Adam Miller, Amen Street Fish & Raw Bar | Charleston, South Carolina

Amen Street's name is inspired by an eighteenth-century stretch of road between East Bay and Church Street where the faithfuls' amens rang out every Sunday from St. Philip's Episcopal Church and the Methodist Meeting House. Amen, indeed: All the food I've tried here is praiseworthy. This appetizer is a quartet of flavors: the heat of the shrimp playing in savory melody with a black-eyed pea vinaigrette and tomato fondue, harmonizing with a sweeter cornbread that counteracts the shrimp's seasoning and vinaigrette's acidity. This is an original gathering of tastes and textures that's wholly rooted in its region's earth. Chef Adam Miller calls it a "scream of Southern"; he's lived in South Carolina since he was a kid, so understands the Lowcountry's symphony of flavors. It's a recipe that is actually four recipes—but it's *so* worth the time.

Serves 4

INGREDIENTS

24 large shrimp, peeled and deveined

¼ cup vegetable oil

2 to 4 tablespoons blackening seasoning (depending on heat preference)

4 pieces of Sweet Cornbread (see recipe, page 233)

1 cup Tomato Fondue, at room temperature (see recipe, page 45)

1 cup Black-Eyed Pea Vinaigrette Salad (see recipe, page 234)

PROCESS

1 Toss the shrimp, oil, and blackening seasoning in a bowl; set aside to marinate for 15 minutes.

2 Cook the shrimp on an outdoor grill or in a well-seasoned cast-iron skillet until opaque.

3 Spoon a puddle of the warm tomato fondue onto each plate or shallow bowl; top with a piece of cornbread off to the side. Place six of the cooked shrimp on top of the fondue; stir the black-eyed pea vinaigrette and spoon it over the shrimp and cornbread. Serve immediately.

four

Light Fare

Soups, Salads & Sandwiches

The range of shrimp's possibilities is nowhere more apparent than with soups, salads, and sandwiches. Whether for a brunch, lunch, or supper, there's something here for every palate. Keep in mind that many of these dishes can be prepared with leftover shrimp from a feast.

Surfcasting in stormy seas near North Beach's jetty, Tybee Island, Georgia.

Old School Shrimp Salad

There are as many variations on shrimp salad as there are southerners, it seems. Some people include a whisper of sherry, some prefer shredded cabbage or jicama to celery, some punch it up with intense spicing, and others add more exotic ingredients. For me, shrimp salad needs to taste like shrimp, so I like to keep things simple. I cannot abide tarragon and other taste invaders. I use half low-fat mayonnaise and half low-fat sour cream to cut the calories back (and because I don't love mayonnaise). I like the sweeter white shrimp best for a delicately flavored salad.

Serves 2 as a main course

INGREDIENTS

1 pound medium shrimp, steamed, shelled, and deveined, still warm

1 tablespoon fresh lemon juice

½ teaspoon distilled white vinegar

½ teaspoon seafood boil spice, or more to taste

Dash of celery seed

⅓ cup mayonnaise (reduced fat is fine)

⅓ cup sour cream (reduced fat is fine)

⅓ cup thinly sliced celery

½ small red bell pepper, diced (optional)

¼ cup finely diced red onion (optional)

2 ripe avocados

PROCESS

1 Slice each shrimp in half lengthwise.

2 Whisk the lemon juice, vinegar, seafood boil spice, celery seed, mayonnaise, and sour cream together in a large bowl. Add the shrimp, celery, bell pepper, and onion (if desired) and toss to coat. Cover and refrigerate until ready to serve.

3 Cut the avocados in half; remove pits. Use half an avocado for each appetizer serving, filling with shrimp.

Tip: Lydell "Delly" Easton of Rockville, South Carolina, suggests bruising each shrimp between your thumb and finger while still warm to break up the meat, allowing it to absorb flavors more easily.

Photo by Charity Burggraaf.

Sautéed Shrimp

Chef George Spriggs, North Beach Grill | Tybee Island, Georgia

Chef Spriggs tops salads with these shrimp; you can incorporate them into omelets, tacos, burritos, grits, and lots of other dishes.

Serves 2 to 4

INGREDIENTS

1 tablespoon olive oil

1 pound medium shrimp, shelled and deveined

1 tablespoon minced garlic

2½ tablespoons Cajun seasoning

⅓ cup shrimp or fish stock (see page 25)

2 tablespoons butter

PROCESS

1 Place a sauté pan over high heat and allow to heat for about 1 minute. Add the oil to pan, followed by the shrimp.

2 Toss or stir the shrimp until the first signs of pink coloring appear, then add the garlic.

3 Continue to toss the shrimp for 30 seconds, then add the Cajun seasoning and stock. Allow the shrimp to simmer and the liquid to reduce until the shrimp are cooked through. Add the butter just before the shrimp are done to help thicken sauce.

Overleaf: Jared Keefe (*left*) and Charles "The Shrimp Pimp" Riley haul, sort, and head shrimp aboard Captain Roy Woodard's *Las Ninas II*. Woodard is a Tybee native who's been shrimping for more than fifty years. Photo by Jay Fleming.

Shrimp, Avocado, and Tomato Trifle with Wasabi Cream

To make this salad more of a true trifle, you can double the cream dressing and include a layer of crumbled cornbread or biscuits halfway up the bowl.

Serves 6

INGREDIENTS

½ cup light sour cream

½ cup mayonnaise (reduced fat is fine)

1 teaspoon wasabi paste or powder

Juice of ½ lime

4 tomatoes, squeezed free of seeds, diced

4 ripe avocados, diced

1 pound medium shrimp, steamed in seafood boil spice and shelled

Salt and freshly ground black pepper to taste

PROCESS

1 Whisk the sour cream, mayonnaise, wasabi, and lime juice together in a bowl.

2 In a trifle or other large, clear glass bowl, layer half of the tomatoes, half of the avocado, then half of the shrimp, sprinkling each layer very lightly with salt and pepper. Pour half of the wasabi dressing over the shrimp, then repeat the layering and top with the remaining dressing.

3 When serving, dig down into the bottom of the bowl with salad tongs to pull up a good mix of ingredients for each person.

Shrimp and Cucumber
Tea Sandwiches

After suffering through one too many tasteless cucumber sandwiches, I was forced to come up with my own recipe. Honestly, do you think you can merely slice a cucumber, butter some bread, smack it all together, and call it a day? No. Here's the flavorful way, with shrimp added for color and fun. Assemble these minutes before your guests arrive—and do not skip patting the shrimp and cucumber slices dry! Otherwise you'll have a sodden mess on your hands instead of a dainty, delicious, old-fashioned treat.

Makes 16 pieces

INGREDIENTS

1 cucumber, peeled and thinly sliced (about ⅛ inch) into at least 16 rounds

1 cup cider vinegar

8 ounces (1 package) cream cheese, softened

¼ cup mayonnaise

½ teaspoon onion powder

¼ teaspoon garlic powder

¼ teaspoon salt

¼ teaspoon white pepper

2 tablespoons fresh snipped fresh dill

8 extra-thin slices white bread, crusts removed

8 medium shrimp, steamed in seafood boil spice, deveined and shelled, and cut in half lengthwise

PROCESS

1 Soak the cucumber slices in the vinegar and 2 cups water for 30 minutes.

2 While the cucumber slices are marinating, mix the cream cheese, mayonnaise, spices, and dill.

3 Drain the cucumber slices; dry them on paper towels, patting as necessary.

4 Slather cream cheese spread onto four of the bread slices to just before their edges; arrange one cucumber slice and one shrimp half in each corner of the bread slices.

5 Top with the remaining bread slices and cut each into four squares. Serve immediately.

Seafood Cocktail

Chef Shawn Kelly, High Cotton | Charleston, South Carolina

A tangy, textured take on seafood salad that's as pretty as it is delicious.

Serves 4

INGREDIENTS

½ cup fresh lemon juice (or combination of other citrus juices such as blood orange or grapefruit)

¼ cup diced shallots

1 teaspoon salt

1 tablespoon sugar

½ teaspoon white pepper

1 cup olive oil

8 large poached or boiled deveined and shelled shrimp, cut in half lengthwise

8 ounces crabmeat, picked over to remove any shells

4 ounces cooked lobster meat

1 avocado, coarsely diced

1 tablespoon toasted pine nuts

3 tablespoons chopped fresh basil (or other herbs such as parsley or tarragon)

PROCESS

1 Stir together, in this order, the lemon juice, shallots, 1 teaspoon salt, the sugar, pepper, and oil. There will be some extra, but this vinaigrette stores well in the refrigerator and can be used as a dressing or a marinade.

2 In a bowl, toss together the seafood, avocado, pine nuts, basil, and salt to taste with enough of the dressing to coat. Taste, and add more vinaigrette if needed. Serve immediately.

Overleaf: Cotton bolls and pod near Darlington, South Carolina.

Tom Kha Gai

Kimberly Killebrew, The Daring Gourmet | www.daringgourmet.com

On her blog, Kimberly relays the Thai people's love of food through their common greeting: "Gin khao reu yung?" which means "Have you eaten yet?" Tom kha gai is a classic Thai dish with a wonderful aroma and comforting flavor.

Serves 4

INGREDIENTS

½ tablespoon coconut oil

1½ tablespoons Thai red curry paste (can be found in Asian markets)

3 cups strong chicken, vegetable, or shrimp stock

3 cups unsweetened coconut milk

1 large lemongrass stalk, trimmed and cut into 2-inch pieces

6 thin slices fresh galangal or ginger

2 Thai bird chiles, seeded and very thinly sliced (use less if you prefer it less spicy)

3 tablespoons fresh lime juice

2 tablespoons Asian fish sauce

1 pound medium-large shrimp, shelled and deveined

1 cup white button mushrooms, thinly sliced

¼ cup fresh basil leaves (preferably Thai basil), thinly sliced

Salt to taste (optional)

Fresh cilantro or more basil leaves for garnish

PROCESS

1 Warm the oil in a soup pot over medium heat. Add the curry paste and cook, stirring, until fragrant, 3 minutes or so.

2 Add the stock, coconut milk, lemongrass, galangal, chiles, lime juice, and fish sauce. Bring to a simmer and cook for 5 minutes.

3 Add the shrimp and simmer for 15 minutes.

4 Add the mushrooms and basil and simmer for another 5 minutes; add salt to taste if needed.

5 Remove and discard the lemongrass and galangal and serve immediately, garnished with cilantro or more basil.

Shrimp and Watermelon Salad

Chef Joel St. John, St. John's Fire Food Truck | Houston, Texas

This is a beautiful and unexpected combination that's perfect on a hot summer day.

Serves 6

INGREDIENTS

1 cup olive oil

1 cup whole chiles de árbol

1½ pounds small shrimp, peeled and deveined

Seafood boil spice

1 red onion, thinly sliced

1 bunch watercress, chopped

1 small bunch mint, chopped

12 cups seedless watermelon cut into 1-inch cubes

PROCESS

1 Put the oil and chiles in a saucepan and heat over medium heat until the chiles start to simmer; remove from the heat. Using a slotted spoon, remove the chiles from the oil. Discard the chiles (or save them for another use) and set the oil aside.

2 Poach the shrimp in simmering water seasoned with seafood boil spice until pink, 3 to 5 minutes, then drain and chill in an ice water bath.

3 Toss together the onion, watercress, mint, watermelon, and shrimp in a bowl; cover and refrigerate until cold.

4 Drizzle some of the chile oil over the salad and serve on small plates.

Savage Storms, Salving Trees

The Gulf Coast's Transformed Remains of Hurricane-Toppled Live Oak Trees

Driving along the Gulf of Mexico's rim from Bay St. Louis to Biloxi, Mississippi, you'll see large wooden sculptures of angels with outstretched wings, leaping dolphins, and graceful herons. If you didn't know better, you'd think they were simply pretty folk art presences in these resort towns. You wouldn't realize that those sculptures are actually shouts of resilience following Hurricane Katrina's destruction of thousands of live oak trees with their iconic Spanish moss "beards." What you now see as an angel's wings were once limbs that soared heavenward.

In Galveston, Texas, Hurricane Ike wiped out an estimated forty thousand trees in 2008. The island is no stranger to devastating hurricanes, given its history with the cataclysmic event in 1900 that came to be known as Isaac's Storm for the Weather Bureau employee, Isaac Cline, who documented the wrath that claimed six thousand souls, including that of his wife.

carved a conch-calling mermaid surrounded by leaping dolphins, inspired by the mother at the tree's home whose children used to climb up and hide in it, forcing her to yell out for them for dinner. Jim Phillips's train conductor near the Galveston Railroad Museum has beads of sap on the tips of his nose and chin as if he's sweating in the cloying humidity of a Gulf summer.

The remains of many trees were milled for siding and floors for the reconstruction effort. The downed trees also provided twenty thousand tons of lumber for the S.S. *Charles W. Morgan*, a whaling ship docked at Mystic, Connecticut's seaport; live oaks, because of their curving limbs, were historically used in boat building. Galveston's Chamber of Commerce gifted ten thousand live oak saplings to the island's citizens, so one day the twisting limbs and swaying moss shall rise again to grace the town.

The sculptures are a classic example of making lemonade from lemons, but beyond that, they're testaments to the strength of community after tragedies and to the power of art to lift spirits. Those chain saws and chisels transformed more than individual trunks and limbs of injured trees. ❧

Donna Leibbert, a resident in Galveston's historic district, lived with the wounds Ike inflicted on all of these grand trees, some hundred-year-old "century oaks." She mourned the stricken beings whose leaves and limbs were stripped by his fierce breath and then poisoned by the chemical-laden Back Bay water surge. Inspired by similar work in New Orleans after Katrina, she made it her business to shake a fist at Ike by arranging for carvers to resurrect the scarred remains into scores of sculptures. Galveston-born Earl Jones

Panzanella Shrimp Salad

Chef Chaka Garcia, Farley Girls | Galveston, Texas

I've had so many tasty shrimp dishes over the years, but this bread salad is one that I wish I could dig into at least once a week. If I lived in Galveston, I'd definitely be a regular at Farley Girls! Grilled chicken or boiled crawfish can be used in place of the shrimp.

Serves 2

INGREDIENTS

1 cup 1-inch cubes of Texas toast, sourdough, or baked pizza crust

1 cup olive oil

4 teaspoons minced garlic

3 basil leaves, cut chiffonade

½ teaspoon cracked pepper

½ teaspoon sea salt

½ cup diced Roma tomato

½ cup diced seeded cucumber

¼ to ½ cup minced red onion

½ cup crumbled feta cheese

½ cup grilled medium shrimp

1 teaspoon seafood boil spice, plus more for garnish

¼ cup light blue cheese dressing

1 teaspoon chopped fresh parsley

PROCESS

1 Toss the cubed bread with the oil, garlic, basil, cracked pepper, and salt.

2 Spread the bread cubes in a baking pan and bake for 5 minutes at 350°F; let cool completely.

3 Toss the bread cubes in a large bowl with the tomato, cucumber, onion, cheese, shrimp, and seafood boil spice.

4 Add the dressing, tossing to coat all ingredients.

5 Sprinkle with seafood boil spice and parsley and serve immediately.

Chilled Shrimp and Cucumber Soup

Dolores Hall, from Frances Schultz's *Atlanta at Table* | Atlanta, Georgia

As the ever-lovely Frances mentions in her book, from lowly canned soup or bisque comes this refreshing, but substantial, summer delight.

Serves 8 as a main course

INGREDIENTS

4 medium cucumbers

Salt

12 ounces shrimp, cooked, shelled, deveined, and chopped

2 cups canned tomato soup or bisque

2 cups chicken stock

6 cups plain yogurt (reduced fat is fine)

2 cups whipping cream or reduced-fat milk

4 cloves garlic, crushed

Chopped fresh parsley

PROCESS

1 Peel, seed, and dice the cucumbers; sprinkle with salt, let stand for 30 minutes, then rinse and pat dry.

2 Combine the cucumbers, shrimp, tomato soup, stock, yogurt, cream, and garlic; cover and refrigerate until chilled.

3 Sprinkle with parsley before serving.

Tip: I make my chicken stock from rotisserie chicken leftovers, which offer a deeper flavor.

Gardenia in a spring rain, Christ Church Cemetery, St. Simons Island, Georgia.

Shrimp Rangoon
Grilled Cheese Sandwiches

Dax Phillips, Simple Comfort Food | www.simplecomfortfood.com

Grilled cheese meets stuffed wontons . . . nomnomnom.

Makes 4 sandwiches

INGREDIENTS

1 pound cooked shrimp, shelled and
 deveined

½ cup thinly sliced scallions

1 teaspoon soy sauce

1 teaspoon Worcestershire sauce

1 teaspoon cracked pepper

8 ounces (1 package) cream cheese, at
 room temperature

8 slices ciabatta bread, each lightly
 buttered on one side

PROCESS

1 Pulse the shrimp in a food processor a few times to break it up a little.

2 Stir together the shrimp, scallions, soy and Worcestershire sauces, pepper, and cream cheese, folding until everything is nicely mixed.

3 Heat a cast-iron skillet over medium heat. Lay the first slice of bread, butter side down, into the skillet.

4 Generously add the shrimp mixture, then top with the other slice of bread, butter side up. Cook each side until the bread is golden and repeat to make three more sandwiches.

Photo by Charity Burggraaf.

Cajun Gumbo

Jack Collins | Brownsville, Texas

Another gift from the "shrimp basin" of Brownsville. My thanks to Tony Reisinger for sharing the culinary creations of his industry friends. Many grocery store chains sell gumbo filé seasoning, but if yours doesn't, it's easy to find through online retailers. Filé is a sassafras powder that's used to thicken the gumbo; in a pinch, some people let the okra do the thickening, or use some roux paste.

Serves 10 to 12

INGREDIENTS

1 bunch scallions

1 large yellow or white onion

3 stalks celery

1 green bell pepper

1 link smoked sausage

½ cup cooking oil

¾ cup all-purpose flour

3 to 4 pounds shrimp (60- to 70-count), steamed and peeled (or roasted chicken, or a combination)

3 teaspoons garlic powder

3 teaspoons freshly ground black pepper

Salt to taste

3 teaspoons gumbo filé

1 pound frozen sliced okra (optional)

2 teaspoons hot sauce

Hot cooked rice

PROCESS

1 Chop the scallions, onion, celery, and bell pepper; cut the sausage into medium-thin slices.

2 Heat the oil in heavy stew pot over medium-high heat. Add the flour and cook, stirring with a whisk, until light brown, about 3 minutes.

3 Add 2 cups water gradually, stirring constantly until a sauce forms.

4 Add the chopped vegetables and simmer for about 15 minutes.

5 Add the sausage and shrimp and simmer for 5 minutes.

6 Add 5 quarts water; bring to a boil.

7 Add the garlic powder, black pepper, filé, and hot sauce, bring back to a slow boil, then add okra, if desired, and simmer for 1½ to 2 hours, until thick like a stew. Serve over rice.

Spicy Beer and Butter Shrimp with
Cornbread Crouton Salad

Tieghan Gerard, Half Baked Harvest | www.halfbakedharvest.com

I flat-out drooled when I first read this recipe. Then I actually whipped up a batch . . . wow. It's a good thing there's some kick in here, otherwise I'd inhale this. So delicious, and with great texture.

Serves 4

SALAD INGREDIENTS

3 cups cubed Sweet Honey Jalapeño
  Cheddar Cornbread (see recipe, page
  232)
3 tablespoons olive oil
Salt and freshly ground black pepper
  to taste
Juice of 2 limes
1 teaspoon honey
1 canned chipotle chile in adobo sauce,
  minced
2 tablespoons chopped fresh cilantro,
  plus more for garnish
8 cups spring greens
1 pint grape tomatoes, halved
Kernels from 1 ear grilled corn
1 avocado, diced
8 ounces cubed sharp cheddar cheese

SHRIMP INGREDIENTS

4 tablespoons butter
1 pound peeled and deveined shrimp
¾ cup beer—whatever your favorite
  brand is
1 clove garlic, minced or grated
2 teaspoons smoked paprika
2 teaspoons brown sugar
1 teaspoon cayenne pepper
1 teaspoon chili powder
¼ teaspoon salt
½ teaspoon freshly ground black pepper

PROCESS

1 Preheat the oven to 450°F.

2 Grease a baking sheet and spread the cornbread on it in a single layer; drizzle with 1 tablespoon of the oil and sprinkle with salt and pepper. Carefully toss the cornbread, making sure not to let the bread crumble into small pieces.

3 Toast in the oven for 7 to 10 minutes, turning once, or until the cubes are browned.

4 While the cornbread bakes, work on the shrimp: Heat a large skillet over medium-high heat; add the butter.

5 Add the shrimp, beer, garlic, smoked paprika, brown sugar, cayenne pepper, chili powder, salt, and pepper. Bring to a boil, then reduce to a simmer. Simmer until the shrimp is cooked through and the sauce has thickened and reduced down to about ⅓ cup, about 10 minutes; stir the shrimp 3 or 4 times while cooking.

6 For the salad, in a small bowl, whisk together the remaining 2 tablespoons oil, the lime juice, honey, chipotle, and cilantro. Season with salt and pepper.

7 To assemble the salad, place the greens, tomatoes, corn, and avocado in a large bowl. Add as much of the dressing as you would like and toss well.

8 Divide the salad among four plates or bowls. Top each plate with equal amounts of cornbread croutons and cheese. Finally, divide the shrimp among the salads, adding sauce as well, if desired. Serve immediately.

Carolina Shrimp and She-Rock Stew

Harry Glyn Jarvis Jr. | Williamsburg, Virginia

The Jarvis family is well known in coastal North Carolina for their grandfather, Captain Harry Jackson Jarvis, and his famous restaurant Captain Harry's, as well as the family's seafood processing plants. Harry Glyn Jarvis Sr. owns the Oyster Creek Marina. Seafood—and its many manifestations through great recipes—is in the family's blood!

This makes a big batch, but it freezes well.

Serves 12

INGREDIENTS

1 cup (2 sticks) butter

1 tablespoon Cajun seasoning

4 teaspoons seafood boil spice

1 tablespoon freshly ground black pepper

2 teaspoons paprika

1 tablespoon sugar

¾ cup dry sherry

1 leek, white part only, well rinsed, diced

4 stalks celery, diced

1 large sweet onion (Vidalia or Walla Walla), diced

2 tablespoons salt (for boiling fish)

2 pounds rockfish fillets (striped bass or other white fish), cut into 1- to 2-inch chunks

1 pound large white shrimp, shelled and deveined

1 quart whole milk

1 quart half-and-half

1½ cups all-purpose flour

PROCESS

1 In large stockpot, melt the butter over medium-high heat, then add the seasonings and sherry, stirring until mixed.

2 Add the leek, celery, and onion and continue to cook over high heat, stirring often, until the vegetables caramelize, 5 to 7 minutes.

3 Fill a separate stockpot with water and add the salt; bring to a boil. Add the fish and shrimp and cook for 5 minutes.

4 Drain the fish and shrimp, reserving 2 cups of the stock.

5 Flake the fish with fork until it's the consistency of crabmeat.

6 Add the flour to the vegetable mixture, stirring over medium-high heat to make a roux paste.

7 Add the stock gradually, stirring until a smooth sauce forms.

8 Add the milk and half-and-half and continue to stir until it thickens.

9 Add the cooked fish and serve.

Mexican Shrimp, Black Bean, and Corn Salad

This is a perfect use for leftover shrimp and corn on the cob.   **Serves 4**

INGREDIENTS

1 cup steamed and peeled shrimp (a little more or less doesn't matter)

1 (11-ounce) can shoepeg corn, drained; or about 1½ cups leftover corn cut from the cob

½ green bell pepper, finely diced

½ red or orange bell pepper, finely diced

½ cup diced cucumber

3 tablespoons finely diced red onion

1 (14-ounce) can black beans, drained and well rinsed

4 teaspoons ground cumin

½ cup fresh lime juice

½ teaspoon salt

½ cup olive oil

3 teaspoons hot sauce, or to taste

¼ cup chopped fresh cilantro

PROCESS

1 Cut the shrimp into bite-sized pieces, if large.

2 Combine the shrimp and all the remaining ingredients and set aside to marinate for at least 1 hour, or longer in the refrigerator, tossing a few times. Serve chilled or at room temperature.

A "Free Range" Shrimper

Captain Joseph Andrews III of the *Gray Ghost*, Engelhard and Ocracoke, North Carolina

Fishermen are by nature an independent lot; images of a lone fly fisherman in a Montana river, a surfcaster on an Atlantic beach, or a single form casting from a canoe on a misty lake all come to mind. But of the many trawler captains I've met who give off a "my way" vibe, Captain Joe Andrews outloners them all.

From Brownsville, Texas, to the villages along North Carolina's Pamlico Sound, dock after dock is lined with bright white trawlers, if not three and four deep as they once were in these harbors. I saw a yellow trawler in Rockville, South Carolina, and a black one moored at Tarpon Springs, Florida, but the boat that stood out the most in my travels is the *Gray Ghost*. Its faded Stars and Bars tells you she's a Confederate homage of some sort; specifically, the nod is to the cavalry officer John S. Mosby of the 43rd Virginia Batallion, whose nickname was the Gray Ghost.

In Captain Andrews's case (a sergeant with the Seventh North Carolina reenactor's group), the name also represents an affinity to the men in Mosby's command, the Rangers who were known for their effective strikes on Union targets and their stealthy ability to escape detection. "I'm what you'd call a free-range shrimper," Andrews told me. "I don't want nobody lookin' over my shoulder. I work alone, sellin' direct to chefs, families, and markets. I don't care to be seen or heard, so my gray boat means people can't see me out on the water with the naked eye like they can a glarin' white boat, and other shrimpers can't follow after me tryin' to catch in my spots."

Andrews rebuilt his boat, originally rigged for drop net fishing, into a trawler, bringing a 1943 671 gray marine engine—still sporting its leather fuel pump seals—up to grade in the process. "I'm a vintage guy. I don't want some engine with all sorts of technology that I can't fix myself. I want somethin' simple I can take apart, and these engines were used in World War II in the amphibious boats that landed at Normandy." On a good trip over a couple days, he can haul in more than a thousand pounds of shrimp—a considerable amount for someone "buggin'" alone—so the repairs and his strategies clearly serve him well.

Andrews docks in Engelhard, where his family's been in commercial fishing for generations, but also shrimps in the Outer Banks and sells on Ocracoke, where he's been visiting and working since he was twelve. "I don't wanna be around all the jabberin' and yammerin' at the bigger company docks where there are eighty boats lined up. I want to stay the hell away from all that rush. I'd rather sell right to the people I growed up with on Ocracoke who know me, who ride away with a bag of my shrimp on their handlebars with extra ice 'cause it's a long peddle back to their cottage." ✤

Chimichurri Shrimp Salad

Chef Ari Kolender, Leon's Oyster Shop | Charleston, South Carolina

Chef Kolender, a James Beard Rising Star Chef of the Year semifinalist, also serves this dish as a "chunky shrimp dip" with crackers or prawn chips found at Asian food markets.

Serves 4, with leftover sauce and pickled onions

CHIMICHURRI SAUCE INGREDIENTS

½ cup minced shallots

4 to 6 cloves garlic, peeled

¼ cup seeded and chopped jalapeño pepper

3 tablespoons salt

½ cup chopped fresh cilantro

¼ cup chopped fresh parsley

1 teaspoon fresh oregano leaves

2 tablespoons fresh mint leaves cut into chiffonade

¾ cup red wine vinegar

1¼ cups olive oil

PICKLED RED ONIONS INGREDIENTS

4 red onions

1 quart red wine vinegar

1 tablespoon salt

¾ cup sugar

2 tablespoons chili paste

SALAD INGREDIENTS

1 pound large shrimp, cooked, shelled, deveined, and chilled

¼ cup drained capers, chopped

2 avocados, cut into chunks

1 yellow grapefruit, peeled and cut into segments between the membranes

2 jalapeño peppers, thinly sliced into rings, seeds removed

4 sprigs fresh mint, torn into large pieces

Salt to taste

CHIMICHURRI SAUCE PROCESS

1 In a food processor, combine the shallots, garlic, jalapeño pepper, and salt; chop as finely as possible.

2 Add the herbs, working in batches if necessary.

3 Transfer the mixture to a bowl; slowly whisk in the vinegar and then the oil. Cover and refrigerate immediately to preserve the color; the sauce will keep for at least 1 week in the refrigerator.

PICKLED RED ONIONS PROCESS

1 Slice the onions ¼ inch thick and put them in a heatproof glass or ceramic container.

2 Bring the remaining ingredients to a boil in a saucepan and pour over the onions.

3 Cover and let cool to room temperature, then refrigerate (they'll keep for at least 1 month).

SALAD PROCESS

Mix all the ingredients with ½ cup of the chimichurri sauce and ¼ cup chopped pickled onions; add salt to taste. Serve immediately.

Shrimp Benedict with Lime Hollandaise

This is one of the many elegant disguises for leftover steamed shrimp. For a different zing, try using tart yellow grapefruit juice for the hollandaise sauce; you can always use the traditional lemon juice, too, if you prefer.

Serves 4

INGREDIENTS

3 large egg yolks

¼ cup fresh lime juice

½ cup (1 stick) butter, softened

4 English muffins, biscuits, or Polenta
   Cakes (see recipe, page 219)

2 medium ripe heirloom tomatoes

Salt and white pepper

24 medium to large steamed shrimp,
   peeled and deveined

Seafood boil spice

PROCESS

1 To make the hollandaise sauce, vigorously whisk the egg yolks and lime juice in the top of a double boiler off the heat. Add the butter, whisk again, and place the pot over boiling water. Stir constantly until the butter melts and the sauce thickens, 2 to 3 minutes or until desired consistency; remove from the heat and lift the top pan from the bottom. Set aside.

2 Split and toast the muffins or biscuits, or fry the polenta cakes.

3 Slice the tomatoes ¼ inch thick and sprinkle with salt and white pepper.

4 Layer the tomato slices and a few shrimp on muffin or biscuit halves or polenta cakes; top with the hollandaise sauce and sprinkle with seafood boil spice. Serve immediately.

Shrimp and Sausage Strata

Strata is a perfect brunch or holiday breakfast dish because you prepare it the night before and cook it before guests arrive or as the family awakens. It's inexpensive but presents as a "special occasion" recipe. This is another great use for leftover shrimp.

Serves 8 to 10

INGREDIENTS

10 ounces sliced mushrooms

3 tablespoons butter

8 ounces loose Italian sausage

6 large eggs, beaten

1½ cups milk

1 cup half-and-half

2 cups shredded sharp cheddar cheese

1 teaspoon English mustard powder

2 tablespoons very thinly sliced scallion greens

¼ teaspoon freshly ground black pepper

8 cups seasoned stuffing cubes (or stale bread cut into cubes)

8 ounces steamed shrimp, shelled, deveined, and cut in half lengthwise

PROCESS

1 Sauté the mushrooms in the butter in a single layer in a large skillet until tender and golden, then turn to brown the other sides. Remove from the pan and set aside.

2 Fry the sausage in the pan over medium-high heat until crisp, breaking it up into small pieces as it cooks; set aside.

3 Whisk together the eggs, milk, half-and-half, cheese, mustard powder, scallions, and pepper.

4 Add stuffing cubes, shrimp, cooled mushrooms, and sausage.

5 Grease two 8-inch square glass baking or ceramic casserole dishes and divide the mixture between them. Cover and refrigerate overnight.

6 Take the dishes from the refrigerator 30 minutes before baking.

7 Cook, uncovered, at 350°F for 30 to 40 minutes, until browned on top. Serve hot.

five

Saucy Shrimp

Crown your favorite savory canvas of biscuits, rice, grits, polenta cakes, pastry shells, pizza crusts, toast points, mashed potatoes, savory waffles, cornbread, or pasta with these shrimp sauces. Or, skip the carbs and think of them as delicious stews. Many of these preparations could also be made with chicken, mild fish, or even pork or steak.

"Boat to belly" is Rusty Bellies' take on "farm to table," Tarpon Springs, Florida.

Shrimp and Grits

Pinkney Venning Mikell, Peters Point Plantation | Edisto Island, South Carolina

The Mikells are an honored Edisto Island family whose blood pulses with the ebb and flow of the tidal creeks. Mikells began planting in this soil in the 1600s, and they've been doing so ever since—and on this specific stretch of land along St. Pierre's Creek since 1715. I wasn't surprised when Pinkney offered a shrimp and grits recipe when I asked if he might contribute his tastebuds' wisdom to this collection—what could be more true to his island? In his words, this is a "pantry" dish that's "close to the ground"—uncomplicated and pulled together from ingredients commonly on hand. Shrimp and grits are eaten for breakfast, lunch, and dinner along the southern coasts.

Serves 2 to 4

INGREDIENTS

1 cup good-quality grits

1 cup shrimp stock or water

Salt to taste

1 cup milk

Slosh of whipping cream

½ to 1 pound thick, not-too-smoky bacon

2 to 3 cloves garlic, minced

¼ cup minced onion

2 pounds small raw shrimp, peeled (creek shrimp are best but are hard to find)

¼ cup ketchup

Worcestershire sauce

Hot sauce or cayenne pepper, if desired

4 tablespoons butter

PROCESS

1 In a heavy saucepan, bring the grits, stock, salt, and milk to a boil, then lower the heat and simmer for 20 minutes. (Grits can be cooked longer, if desired; they become more tender.) Stir in the cream and continue to cook the grits slowly, stirring often, for about 10 minutes.

2 In a skillet, fry the bacon until crisp. Remove the bacon to paper towels to drain, decanting the grease into a heatproof container but leaving several tablespoons of the grease in the pan with all the brown crunchy bits.

3 Set the pan over low heat and add the garlic and onion. Cook until they sweat and are soft but not fried.

4 Increase the heat to medium and add the shrimp; cook quickly, turning the shrimp as needed for even heating, but do not cook through—cook just until the shrimp start to take on a pink shade throughout. You will still see some uncooked shrimp.

5 As the pink starts to predominate, add the ketchup and stir to coat shrimp. Add a few dashes of Worcestershire sauce and hot sauce as desired. Salt and freshly ground black pepper can also be added to taste.

6 Continue to cook for another minute, until the shrimp are just cooked through. Remove from the heat and stir in the cold butter, which makes everything glossy and smooth.

7 Spoon the grits into a serving dish or individual dishes, then spoon the shrimp over the top. Crumble the bacon on top and serve.

Scott Dantzler's vintage washing machine tub serves as a fire pit for a winter party at Peters Point Plantation on Edisto Island, South Carolina.

Shrimp 'n' Gravy

Madge Jarvis Williams, Hobo Seafood | Swanquarter, North Carolina

Madge and her husband, Lee, are the proud owners of Hobo Seafood and a fleet of trawlers in Swanquarter. Madge's family has been in the seafood business for generations; her grandfather was Harry Jackson Jarvis, famous for his restaurant, Captain Harry's, and seafood processing plants in the '50s to '70s. Shrimp and gravy is the single most common recipe trawler captains relayed to me; it's what they prepare out on the water and for their families at home.

Serves 4

INGREDIENTS

1 cup chopped raw bacon (roughly 8 ounces, depending on thickness)

1 small onion, finely chopped

2 tablespoons all-purpose flour

¾ cup milk

½ cup beef broth

1 teaspoon garlic powder

Salt and freshly ground black pepper to taste

1 pound small to medium shrimp, peeled and deveined

Hot cooked rice or biscuits

PROCESS

1 Cook the bacon in a large skillet over medium-high heat until crisp. With a slotted spoon, remove the bacon to a plate.

2 Lower the heat to medium. Add the onion to the bacon drippings in the pan. Stir and cook until the onion is translucent, 3 to 5 minutes.

3 In a bowl, combine the flour, ¾ cup water, the milk, broth, garlic powder, and salt and pepper. Add to the pan of fried onions, stirring constantly over medium heat until a gravy has formed and become thick, about 5 minutes.

4 Return the bacon to the skillet and add the shrimp. Reduce the heat to low and simmer for 5 to 8 minutes, stirring occasionally, until the shrimp are pink. Serve over rice or biscuits.

Mike Sawyer (*foreground*) and Jon Sturgess bring in the haul from the *Predator* to Hobo Seafood's dock, Swanquarter, North Carolina.

What's in a (Boat) Name?

Careful What Ya Call 'Er!

One of the charms of the trawler docks is their collection of boat names—odes to heroes, lovers, inspirations, and frustrations.

Many men on trawler crews have been working on boats since they were six or seven, moving up the ladder from header to striker to captain. Some go on to become owners of fleets, restaurants, or markets near the docks they were raised on. But when they're starting out, the dream is to own their own boat. Naming the manifestation of those dreams, the source of their livelihoods and identities to a great degree, is no small decision. It's different than naming lake cabins, shore cottages, or pleasure boats that represent an escape from cares. Randy Sawyer, who owns the trawler *Nasty Habit*, says with a wink: "Them yacht owners have the funnier boat names—they have more to be laughing about. Ain't nothin' funny about shrimpin'!"

Boats have a superstition consideration when it comes to naming, too. While most want to make a boat fully their own, having its name reflect their families or personalities or ambitions,

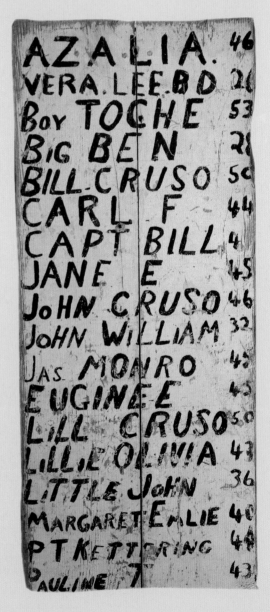

it's considered unlucky to rename it—unless you follow a certain ritual when doing so. Madge Williams, the matriarch of Hobo Seafood in Swanquarter, North Carolina, attests to this: "I believe in that superstition a bit. My husband, Lee, changed the name of one of our boats, the *Master Les*, to *Addiction* in honor of his penchant for salvaging trawlers. I joke that this was bad luck, because that boat has had frequent breakdowns and has an ADDICTION to mechanical work . . . and still often remains . . . MasterLESS!"

Surveying the thousand-plus Gulf and Atlantic offshore trawler names from license lists, the words you'll find most frequently painted on the boats are: Miss, Capt, Lady, Master, Lucky, Sea, and Thanh—a common Vietnamese name, and a nod to the prevalence of trawlers from this community in the Gulf. But as with coffee shops ("Legal Grounds") and hair salons ("Curl up and Dye"), there's an instinct for plays on words in boat naming, too. My favorite, docked in Stumpy Point, North Carolina, and playing on the name of a type of net, sums up the shrimping life: "N-Seine." ❧

Ponchartrain Sauce

Chef Chaka Garcia, Farley Girls | Galveston, Texas

Pontchartrain is a famous New Orleans–area Cajun sauce; Chef Chaka serves his on pasta and as a pizza topping. This is one of those comfort food sauces that you could use just about any meat with, but it complements shrimp perfectly. This is a quick but tasty version of a recipe that can go pages long from other chefs.

Serves 2

INGREDIENTS

½ cup sliced mushrooms

2 tablespoons butter

¼ cup whipping cream

½ cup grilled peeled medium shrimp

½ cup prepared Alfredo sauce

½ teaspoon seafood boil spice

Hot cooked rice or pasta

1 tablespoon chopped fresh curly parsley

¼ cup sliced scallion greens

Grated Parmesan cheese

PROCESS

1 Sauté the mushrooms in the butter in a single layer in a large sauté pan, turning once, until browned, about 10 minutes total; if the mushrooms are stacked, they'll steam and become watery instead of browning.

2 Add the cream and allow it to deglaze pan and come to a rolling boil; reduce the heat to a simmer.

3 Add the shrimp, Alfredo sauce, and seafood boil spice. Bring to a rolling boil.

4 Serve over rice or pasta, topped with the parsley, scallions, and cheese.

Spicy Peanut Butter Shrimp

Chef David Clark, Shrimp Haus | South Padre Island, Texas

The layering of flavors in this sauce is divine, with the punch of the grapefruit juice really taking it to the next level.

Serves 4

INGREDIENTS

2 tablespoons soy sauce

¼ cup brown sugar

½ cup water

1 jalapeño pepper, minced

3 teaspoons grated fresh ginger

1 clove garlic, minced, plus 1 tablespoon minced

¼ cup creamy peanut butter

2 tablespoons fresh grapefruit juice

2 tablespoons fresh lime juice

1 tablespoon minced shallot

1 tablespoon minced fresh chives

¼ cup olive oil

28 large shrimp, shelled and deveined

¼ cup white wine

6 tablespoons unsalted butter

Hot cooked rice

Sliced scallions

PROCESS

1 Bring the soy sauce, brown sugar, and ½ cup water to a boil in a small saucepan; set aside.

2 Put the jalapeño pepper, ginger, and 1 clove garlic in a blender and add the soy sauce mixture. Puree and transfer to a bowl.

3 Stir in the peanut butter and add the grapefruit and lime juices.

4 Sauté the shallot, the remaining 1 tablespoon garlic, and the chives in the oil in a sauté pan over medium heat; add the shrimp, then the wine. When the shrimp turn pink, after about 3 minutes, add the butter.

5 When the butter is incorporated, add the peanut butter sauce and toss together.

6 Serve over rice, sprinkled with scallions.

Overleaf: A trawler comes home at dawn as fishermen head out on the jetty, South Padre Island, Texas.

South Padre Island's "UFO"—a lifeboat that washed ashore from a sunken tanker—is now covered in flattened beer cans, lighters, and other objects left behind by the surf. It's spots like this that have earned the island the nickname "South Party Island."

Shrimp in Jalapeño Pepper Cream Sauce

Chef David Clark, Shrimp Haus | South Padre Island, Texas

Shrimp Haus is a massive restaurant that's connected to Schlitterbahn Beach Resort and Waterpark on South Padre Island, but dishes like this prove that even kitchens that serve hundreds of people at a time can still deliver a fine meal.

Serves 4

INGREDIENTS

7 tablespoons butter

1 tablespoon chopped garlic

1 tablespoon chopped shallot

¼ cup drained pickled jalapeño peppers, minced

¼ cup Shrimp Stock (see recipe, page 25)

1 teaspoon white pepper

1 teaspoon salt

2 tablespoons white wine

1 cup whipping cream

¼ cup grated Parmesan cheese

1 pound large shrimp, shelled and deveined

Polenta Cakes (see recipe, page 219) or hot cooked grits

1 tablespoon minced fresh curly parsley

PROCESS

1 In a heavy saucepan over medium heat, melt 1 tablespoon of the butter and sauté the garlic, shallot, and pickled jalapeño until soft, about 5 minutes.

2 Add the stock, white pepper, salt, and wine. Bring to a boil.

3 When the liquid is reduced by about half, add the cream, then boil until reduced by half again.

4 Stir in the remaining 6 tablespoons butter and the cheese.

5 Add the shrimp and cook until they are opaque, 3 to 5 minutes. Serve over polenta cakes or grits, garnished with the parsley.

Immortalizing Shrimp

Tony Reisinger: Marine Biologist and Gyotaku Artist,
South Padre Island, Texas

Tony Reisinger has salt water running through his veins. He grew up on St. Simons Island in Georgia, where he later worked aboard the research vessel *Anna* studying shrimp. He's lived in Key West and on Amelia Island and now spends time on South Padre Island, Texas, and all parts north and east along the Gulf Coast assisting the shrimping community through Texas A&M's Sea Grant extension program.

Tony works with trawler captains on compliant installation of turtle extractor devices (TEDs) that limit by-catch in the nets, and troubleshoots when there are red tides and other disruptive natural occurrences. He also runs the Texas Coastal Naturalist program for Cameron County, training volunteers to be first responders who help save shore birds, sea turtles, and coastal wildlife from strandings, oil spills, and other life-threatening situations.

But he's just as comfortable in his right brain as he is in his left as a skilled gyotaku artist—the Japanese fish printing where everything from octopi and snapper to, here, Gulf shrimp, are hand painted so their likenesses can be transferred onto rice or mulberry paper. Japanese fishermen used the images as records of catches, similar to the prints of Kobe beef cattle snouts that catalog herds—sort of Japanese fingerprinting. His works are sold mainly to private collectors and the highest bidders at local charity auctions.

My drive along the Gulf of Mexico and Atlantic coasts kicked off with Tony on a beautiful September day. We started out while it was still dark, driving down to the jetty after fueling up on coffee and cinnamon rolls. The trawlers, lights still on, were coming home through Brazos Santiago Pass ("The arms of St. James") while fishermen were heading out on foot, balancing on the slippery rocks carrying their rods, bait buckets, and nets, silhouetted by dawn's lavender and gold glow. From there, we went looking for lucky sea beans in the wrack with only herons as our company, then visited the turtle rescue center and downed

a killer chipotle shrimp for lunch. To crown the day, Tony gave me a gyotaku demonstration—the print from which is the prized possession from my three-thousand-mile journey.

Beyond his significant scientific expertise and artistry, this southern boy is a party in a pickup truck. He's full of stories and routes to cool hidden spots to explore and keeps fantastic aged tequila (in a bottle wrapped in a hand-woven mariner's macrame) in a knapsack. He stands over six feet tall, but Tony still puts the "imp" in *shrimp*. ❧

HNA DE LA LAGUNA

Shrimp St. Jacques

Chef David Clark, Shrimp Haus | South Padre Island, Texas

Chef David Clark went back into his restaurant's recipe archive for this one for me; it's an elegant dish that politely requests that you serve it on your good china.

Serves 2

INGREDIENTS

8 large to jumbo shrimp, shelled and
   deveined
¼ cup sliced mushrooms
4 tablespoons butter
¼ cup white wine
1 tablespoon minced shallot
½ tablespoon minced garlic

¼ cup sliced marinated artichokes
Juice of ½ lemon
6 tablespoons lemon hollandaise sauce
   (see recipe, page 126)
Grated Parmesan cheese
Baked puff pastry shells

PROCESS

1 Preheat the broiler to high.

2 In a sauté pan over medium-high heat, cook the shrimp and mushrooms in 2 tablespoons of the butter, stirring frequently, for 3 minutes.

3 Add the wine, shallot, garlic, artichokes, and lemon juice. Cook until the liquid is reduce by three quarters, then add the remaining 2 tablespoons butter.

4 Transfer to an ovenproof dish and top with the hollandaise sauce. Sprinkle with Parmesan cheese; brown under the broiler.

5 Spoon into puff pastry shells and serve.

An elaborate sand castle created by Andy Hancock along Gulf Boulevard, South Padre Island, Texas.

Poached Shrimp in Puttanesca Sauce

Chef Espy Geissler | Tybee Island, Georgia

Living on Tybee, with nearly year-round access to fresh-caught shrimp, Chef Geissler developed this light and fresh version of puttanesca that's easy to assemble; the sauce does not require cooking.

Serves 6

INGREDIENTS

2 or 3 fresh ripe tomatoes, chopped

1 cup kalamata olives, pitted and halved

½ cup drained capers, chopped

½ cup chopped fresh basil

1 cup chopped fresh flat-leaf parsley

8 tinned anchovy fillets, minced

6 cloves garlic, minced

1 teaspoon red pepper flakes

¼ cup red wine vinegar or sherry vinegar

¾ cup extra-virgin olive oil

2 pounds (26 to 30) shrimp, unpeeled

Favorite spice mix, rub, or blend of herbs

1 pound orzo

½ cup crumbled feta cheese (optional)

PROCESS

1 In a large bowl, combine the tomatoes, olives, capers, basil, parsley, anchovies, garlic, red pepper flakes, vinegar, and oil.

2 To poach the shrimp, fill a medium pot three quarters full of water and bring to a boil; remove from heat, wait 1 to 2 minutes, add the shrimp, and stir gently until they are opaque and cooked through, 2 to 4 minutes. Drain in a colander; season heavily with your favorite spice mix. Let cool and absorb flavors. When cooled, peel the shrimp, leaving the tails on.

3 Add the shrimp to the other ingredients in the bowl, folding gently to coat.

4 Cook the orzo according to the instructions on the package; drain in a sieve and let cool.

5 Add orzo to the shrimp mixture until the balance looks right to you. Add the cheese, if desired, and serve at room temperature.

Sea oats at North Beach, Tybee Island, Georgia.

Shrimp Savannah

Chef Gerald Green, Garibaldi | Savannah, Georgia

Garibaldi is my favorite special-occasion restaurant in Savannah. Its downstairs dining room is sort of midcentury clubby, with black leather booths and dim lighting, while the upstairs is an airy, mirrored hall, like a little visit to Paris. Chef Green has many delicious selections on his menu; this one is almost always in the mix at the table when I visit. Pernod is a classic spirits pairing with shrimp and other fish dishes; this surprisingly quick and easy recipe is great for dining tête-à-tête.

Serves 2

INGREDIENTS

4 tablespoons butter, softened

1 teaspoon minced garlic

8 ounces large shrimp

¼ cup Pernod

3 tablespoons diced button mushrooms

¼ cup whipping cream

Toast points

PROCESS

1 Combine the butter and garlic.

2 Put the shrimp, Pernod, mushrooms, cream, and garlic butter in a sauté pan and bring to a rolling boil; cook until the shrimp are pink and opaque, 3 to 5 minutes.

3 Serve with toast points.

Broom fashioned from palmetto fronds and twine, Ossabaw Island, Georgia.

Mom's Shrimp

Chef Karey Lynn Butterworth, Glow | Rockport, Texas

Glow is a comfy little dollhouse of a restaurant in what was once a boathouse; it has a friendly staff and some dynamite original cocktails. When Chef Butterworth serves her mom's recipe, it brings it all home. She sometimes incorporates sautéed leeks into her mashed potatoes; adding additional fried leeks on top could only be a good thing.

Serves 6

INGREDIENTS

3 tablespoons butter, cubed

1 cup button mushrooms, cleaned and quartered with stems

3 pounds (16- to 20-count) shrimp, peeled and deveined

2 tablespoons minced shallot

1 tablespoon minced garlic

¼ cup Chardonnay

2 cups whipping cream

Sea salt and cracked pepper

Creamy mashed potatoes or cooked pasta

Fresh parsley leaves or butter-fried thinly sliced leeks (white parts only)

PROCESS

1 Heat a large sauté pan over medium-high heat and add the butter. When the butter has melted, add the mushrooms and cook until they're soft and the liquid they've released has been reabsorbed and evaporated, about 5 minutes.

2 Add the shrimp, shallot, and garlic and sauté for 2 minutes. Add the wine and cook for about 2 minutes, until reduced.

3 Add the cream and cook for 3 to 5 minutes, until the cream has reduced and thickened. Add salt and cracked pepper to taste.

4 Serve over mashed potatoes or pasta. Garnish with parsley or fried leeks.

Shrimp Newburg

Jan Gregory Moore | Harkers Island, North Carolina

Shrimp Newburg is one of those recipes that I associate with big-city glamour of a by-gone era, but it suits so many occasions, from brunches to dinners, that it's timeless. Harkers Island, like Smith Island in the Chesapeake Bay and other islands that were settled early but remained cut off from the mainland for centuries, is known for its "Carolina brogue" dialect that carries vestiges of colonial English speech. These coastal residents are known as "hoi toiders" (high tiders).

Serves 4

INGREDIENTS

6 tablespoons butter

2 tablespoons all-purpose flour

1½ cups light cream

2 large egg yolks, beaten

1 cup peeled shrimp cut into bite-sized
   pieces

2 tablespoons dry white wine

¼ teaspoon salt

3 dashes hot sauce

2 teaspoons fresh lemon juice

Puff pastry shells, hot cooked rice, or
   toast points

PROCESS

1 Melt the butter over low heat in a 10-inch skillet; blend in the flour.

2 Increase the heat to medium, add the cream, and cook, stirring constantly, until thick, 5 to 7 minutes.

3 Stir a small amount of the hot cream sauce into the egg yolks, then return the egg mixture to the skillet, mixing well.

4 Cook, stirring constantly, until thick, about 3 minutes.

5 Add the shrimp, wine, salt, hot sauce, and lemon juice.

6 Serve in pastry cups or over rice or toast points.

Mandarin Shrimp

Chef John Smith, Hemingway's | Santa Rosa Island, Florida

Chef Smith recommends this sauce as a pairing for sautéed shrimp, coconut-encrusted fish, and even roasted sweet potato mash.

Serves 4

INGREDIENTS

½ cup (1 stick) butter

½ cup whipping cream

1 cup fresh (not canned) mandarin orange segments (see Note)

1 tablespoon white wine

½ teaspoon red pepper flakes

1 tablespoon powdered sugar

1 pound medium shrimp, steamed, shelled, and deveined

Hot cooked rice or pasta

PROCESS

1 Heat a sauté pan over medium heat, then add the butter and cream; bring to a boil, stirring constantly, then lower the heat and simmer until the sauce starts to thicken, about 5 minutes.

2 Add the orange segments, breaking them up as they're folded into the sauce.

3 Add the wine, red pepper flakes, and powdered sugar. Stir well, and simmer for about 10 minutes. Add the shrimp.

4 Serve over rice or pasta.

Note: Tangerine, pink grapefruit, or clementine segments can be substituted for the mandarin orange.

Overleaf: Finnish architect Matti Suuronen probably didn't envision his Futuro House, originally designed as a transportable ski chalet, as the residence for extraterrestrials. But given the history of UFO sightings on Santa Rosa Island, Florida, it's entirely appropriate here.

Shrimp Creole

Leuveda Willis Campbell | Savannah, Georgia

Leuveda Garner, Mrs. Campbell's daughter, has a palate that's trained to Georgia shrimp after a lifetime along its coast. She once ordered a dish in a Kingsport, Tennessee, restaurant and after one bite declared the shrimp were caught in Savannah waters. Her dinner companions were skeptical, so they called for the chef—who confirmed the shrimp were indeed from Thunderbolt, which sits along the Wilmington River in Georgia's tidal marshes, about 15 minutes from downtown Savannah. For this dish, which her mother served on ordinary days, she makes the sauce a day ahead to allow the flavors to deepen and blend. This makes it a great quick-preparation dish to serve guests.

Serves 8

INGREDIENTS

3 tablespoons olive oil

6 tablespoons chopped onion

½ cup chopped green bell pepper

½ cup chopped celery

2 (14-ounce) cans diced tomatoes

2 teaspoons salt

Pinch of freshly ground black pepper

2 teaspoons paprika

1 teaspoon sugar

1 teaspoon Worcestershire sauce

1 teaspoon distilled white vinegar

2 pounds peeled and deveined large shrimp

Hot cooked rice

PROCESS

1 Heat the oil in a 10-inch sauté pan over medium heat. Sauté the onion, bell pepper, and celery.

2 Add the tomatoes, salt, black pepper, paprika, sugar, Worcestershire sauce, and vinegar. Cook slowly, uncovered, for about 45 minutes, until the sauce is quite thick, stirring occasionally. Let cool and refrigerate overnight.

3 Reheat the sauce over medium-high heat until bubbly; add the shrimp, and cook just until pink, about 2 minutes. Remove from the heat; serve on rice.

Shrimp Wiggle

Shrimp Wiggle is a throwback dish that wins the Silliest Recipe Name contest. The first print version is believed to be Fannie Merritt Farmer's in the 1898 *Boston Cooking-School Cookbook*, which was a basic cream sauce made in an all-the-rage chafing dish with a cup each of tinned shrimp and peas. In 1911, the *Portsmouth Times* referenced the recipe at the center of a crime: a naughty schoolgirl making a forbidden midnight dormitory supper, a rebellion that earned her a suspension. In the '30s it was put forward as a quick meal for mothers or "career girls." I've seen variations in community cookbooks from the '30s through the '70s, especially in New England, but also in the South. It was often served on toast points (I like crisp rye bread) along with a nice crisp salad. It's still easy, and it's still a nice comfort food—tastier with freshly steamed shrimp and vegetables. For a lower-fat version, omit the cheese and substitute tomato juice for the milk to make it a red sauce (and don't use the sherry). If you have some sliced mushrooms, sauté and toss 'em in there too.

INGREDIENTS

4 tablespoons butter, plus more for the casserole dish or ramekins

4 tablespoons all-purpose flour

1½ cups milk

¼ cup plus 1 tablespoon grated Parmesan cheese

½ teaspoon salt

1 cup cooked seasoned shrimp, chopped if large

1 cup 1-inch pieces steamed asparagus or snap or snow peas (strings removed)

1 teaspoon dry sherry (optional)

Sliced sautéed mushrooms (optional)

1 cup bread crumbs

¼ teaspoon white pepper

Paprika or Italian seasoning blend

A promising sign along Maybank Highway on Wadmalaw Island, South Carolina.

PROCESS

1 Preheat the oven to 350°F.

2 Melt 2 tablespoons of the butter in a sauté pan over medium heat. Stir in the flour. Add the milk slowly; cook, stirring frequently, until thickened, about 5 minutes. Add the ¼ cup cheese and stir until it has melted.

3 Add the salt, shrimp, asparagus, sherry (if using), and mushrooms (if using). Pour into a buttered casserole dish or individual ramekins.

4 Melt the remaining 2 tablespoons butter and toss with the bread crumbs to coat. Add 1 tablespoon grated Parmesan cheese and the white pepper. Distribute on top of the shrimp mixture and sprinkle with paprika.

5 Bake for 20 minutes or so, until the sauce is bubbly and the bread crumbs are lightly toasted.

Dill Pesto Shrimp

I invented this pesto version as part of a thus-far failed attempt to create a savory shrimp shortcake recipe, but it's great as a sauté sauce for shrimp. If thinned down with a little more oil, it's also good as a dip for grilled or baked shrimp. Or, toss the uncooked shrimp with half the batch of pesto and thread them onto skewers for grilling.

Serves 4

INGREDIENTS

2½ cups snipped fresh dill (avoid tough stems if possible)

½ cup crumbled feta cheese

½ cup dry-roasted unsalted cashews

½ cup neutral vegetable oil (*not* olive oil—the flavor competes too much), plus more for cooking the shrimp

2 tablespoons fresh lemon juice

2 pounds large uncooked, peeled, and deveined shrimp

Hot cooked rice or pasta

PROCESS

1 Puree the dill, feta, cashews, oil, and lemon juice in a food processor; set aside.

2 Sauté the shrimp in a little oil in a sauté pan over medium-high heat until opaque or orange-pink, 3 to 5 minutes; add the pesto to taste and cook just to heat through. Serve over rice or pasta.

This seafood lover hopes to score a free meal of steamed shrimp at Waldo's in the Driftwood Resort in Vero Beach, Florida, armed only with big eyes and a quiet mew.

Hot Buttered Rum Shrimp

I've had shrimp spiced with clove and other exotic flavors that surprised my tongue. I've had shrimp cooked up with honey or other sweet additions. I've tried lots of shrimp recipes that include booze. So, one cold night while warming up with hot buttered rums with my dear friend Dave, this idea was born. At first I thought it was the rum talking, but as it turns out—after tinkering with a batch using pink Key West shrimp in the New Hampshire woods, of all places—it really is a tasty combination. The sauce is thin, so it coats the shrimp while still allowing their flavor to shine through, and there's enough of it to pour over rice. I like to serve this with steamed sugar snap peas. It's a nice special-occasion treat.

**Serves 4 as an appetizer
(2 as a main course)**

INGREDIENTS

4 tablespoons salted butter, softened

2 tablespoons dark brown sugar

½ teaspoon ground cinnamon

⅛ teaspoon freshly grated nutmeg

¼ teaspoon ground cayenne pepper

½ teaspoon sea salt

1 pound shelled and deveined large
  shrimp

1 to 2 tablespoons dark rum

1 cup cooked short-grain rice, such as
  Arborio

PROCESS

1 Mix the butter, brown sugar, cinnamon, nutmeg, cayenne pepper, and salt in a bowl.

2 Melt the spiced butter in a large, heavy saucepan over medium-high heat.

3 Increase the heat to high and add the shrimp in a single layer; cook until the shrimp are opaque, about 3 minutes, then turn them over.

4 Cook for 1 minute more, then deglaze the pan with the rum. Allow the sauce to bubble, then remove from the heat.

5 Spoon the shrimp and pour the sauce over the rice.

Green Curry Shrimp

Chef Kurtis Schumm, Bờ Biển Hut | Tybee Island, Georgia

Bờ Biển Hut is an adorable walkup restaurant with a straw roof that serves amazing food—about two blocks from the beach. You can make this a vegetarian dish by substituting more vegetables for the shrimp, or try chicken or pork instead.

Serves 4

INGREDIENTS

½ cup green curry paste

2 tablespoons fresh lime juice

2 quarts whipping cream

½ cup unsweetened coconut milk

1 cup minced fresh cilantro

1 tablespoon fish sauce

1 cup minced scallions

1 cup steamed mixed vegetables (chopped carrots, whole snow peas, or what you have)

1 potato, sliced paper thin and fried, roasted, or boiled

24 shelled and deveined large shrimp, grilled or sautéed in a little oil

2 cups hot steamed white rice

PROCESS

1 Over high heat, cook the curry paste until most of its liquid has evaporated.

2 Add the lime juice and cream. Cook until the sauce has thickened a bit, then add all the remaining ingredients except the rice; bring to a boil and serve over the rice.

six

Main Events

To this day, "shrimp for dinner" still feels like something special to me. When we were growing up, we usually only had it on vacations or when company was coming, so it was always "a treat instead of a treatment," as my mother used to say. There's something festive about it, and because it's so versatile, you could truly eat it every day for a year and never make the same recipe twice, so your palate will never be bored. Here are both classic and creative concoctions from a host of regional and international backgrounds to gather folks to your table.

Reflection of the Jekyll Creek dock as seen in a chandelier finial at Latitude 31°, Jekyll Island, Georgia.

Lowcountry Boil

Chef Matthew Raiford, The Hunting Lodge | Little St. Simons Island, Georgia

A Lowcountry boil is an informal social event, much like a crab feast in the Tidewater region or a barbecue in other parts of the country. At the Hunting Lodge, it's served on long picnic tables covered with gingham tablecloths. However you choose to serve it at home, make sure you have cocktail sauce, Dijon mustard, lemon wedges, and plenty of napkins or moistened washcloths on hand.

INGREDIENTS

Salt

Cayenne pepper

Garlic

Bay leaves

Seafood boil spice

Hot sauce

Whole black peppercorns

A few whole cloves

Juice of 2 lemons, or 2 tablespoons distilled white vinegar

2 small Red Bliss potatoes per person

1 carrot, peeled and cut into four pieces, per person

¼ pound kielbasa and/or Italian sausage per person

1 ear of corn, cut in half, per person

1 or 2 crabs per person (optional)

¼ pound raw shell-on shrimp per person

PROCESS

1 Fill a large pot two thirds full of water and bring to a boil on a stove or outdoor gas cooker.

2 Season the water with salt and your choice of the seasonings along with the lemon juice in proportion to the amount of water.

3 Add the potatoes and cook for 10 minutes. Add the carrots and sausage, bring back to a boil, and cook until the potatoes and carrots are almost tender. Add the corn (and crabs, if using). Cook just a little longer, then add the shrimp and cook until opaque, about 3 minutes.

4 Drain off the water. Pour everything into a basket or onto platters and serve.

Debbie Patton tries her luck along Mosquito Creek on Little St. Simons Island, Georgia.

Lemon Shrimp on Asparagus

Frank Kapaun | Ocean Springs, Mississippi

This dish from the Mississippi coast is full of sparkling fresh flavors and is a great choice for anyone following "Paleo" or carbohydrate-free diets.

Serves 4

INGREDIENTS

4 teaspoons extra-virgin olive oil

2 large red bell peppers, diced

2 pounds asparagus, woody sections snapped off, trimmed, and cut into 1-inch lengths

½ teaspoon grated lemon zest

¼ teaspoon salt

5 cloves garlic, minced

1 pound (26- to 30-count) shrimp, peeled and deveined

2 tablespoons fresh lemon juice

2 tablespoons chopped fresh parsley

PROCESS

1 Heat 2 teaspoons of the oil in a large nonstick skillet over medium-high heat. Add the peppers, asparagus, lemon zest, and salt. Cook, stirring occasionally, until the asparagus is just beginning to soften, about 6 minutes. Transfer to a bowl; cover to keep warm.

2 Add the remaining 2 teaspoons oil and the garlic to the pan and cook, stirring, until fragrant, about 30 seconds. Add the shrimp and cook, stirring, for 1 minute.

3 Remove from the heat. Stir in the lemon juice and parsley. Serve the shrimp and sauce over the asparagus medley.

Folks in the Bible Belt testify their faith as a living, breathing element of their daily lives, often in quite personal, original ways. Here, Jerry Nobles pays penance by sharing the word while wheeling a painted PVC cross up and down Beach Boulevard in Biloxi, Mississippi. He stows fresh socks and a t-shirt inside the cross bar.

Shrimp Risotto

Chef Gerald Green, Garibaldi | Savannah, Georgia

This dish is not only a gorgeous presentation (honestly, everything looks elegant in Garibaldi), but because you cook the risotto in advance, it's actually a quick preparation, too, making it a great choice for dinner parties.

Serves 4

INGREDIENTS

4 pieces of prepared risotto (see Note)

Vegetable oil for frying

1 tablespoon garlic butter (softened butter with a little minced garlic added)

12 ounces (21- to 25-count) shrimp, shelled and deveined

4 ounces country ham, finely chopped

1 cup whipping cream

Salt and freshly ground black pepper to taste

1½ tablespoons minced scallion

PROCESS

1 Heat ⅛ inch oil in a skillet over medium-high heat. Add the risotto pieces and cook for 1 to 2 minutes on each side, until crisp at the edges and warmed through. Remove to individual serving plates.

2 Melt the garlic butter in a sauté pan; add the shrimp, ham, and cream. Cook until the shrimp are opaque, about 3 minutes. Add salt and pepper to taste.

3 Pour the shrimp sauce over the risotto, garnish with scallion, and serve.

Note: Cook a batch of plain risotto; pour into a round casserole dish. Chill until cold throughout. Cut into 8 slices; reserve four for the recipe and freeze the rest for later use.

The Good, the Bad, and the Frightening

Captain William Kemp, Tybee Island, Georgia

Captain William Kemp is a fourth-generation commercial fisherman who enjoys his life in Tybee Island's Spanish Hammock neighborhood, appreciates traditions like the Blessing of the Fleet at Darian, and loves being out on the open water. "Being away from civilization, the peace and privacy, the quiet are all great . . . it's just me and one other guy. Every time you go out to the fishing ground, you're experiencing what men have done basically the same way for hundreds of years." That said, he knows the sea is a worthy opponent as well as the source of calm and riches. "It's man against the water to see who wins." A good day is bringing in a thousand pounds of shrimp; a hard day is "when you tear up a bunch of nets, or when what you pay for oil and the crew is more than what you earned."

Captain Kemp knows what it's like to lose a day to a busted engine, to have it be so cold that the shrimp freeze to the deck, and to have the electronics fail when you're out at sea. His boat, the *Christina Leigh*, was sunk one January day; he got the call when he was on his way to a funeral. The boat went aground at low tide on a sandbar after the equipment went up; fog set in, then the surf pounded the boat. "She finally gave up and laid down after seven hours. Right after she sank, the fog lifted." Fortunately, given his family's deep roots in the industry, there was another boat for him to take out to earn his living.

Storms, too, are a regular part of life. "When you're seven or eight miles out, it gets scary—so foggy you can't see the front of the boat, but with waves breaking over the bow. In thunderstorms, lightning pops the water all around and makes it glow orange; it sounds like an explosion when it hits, then like somebody's welding or frying the water—that sizzle. It makes the hair stand up on the back of your neck . . . all the rig metals attract it, then it knocks out electronics, depth finders, and the radio as the antenna gets struck."

Shrimping, like all livelihoods earned out on the open seas, isn't for sissies. The Gulf of Mexico and the Atlantic are famous for their punishing hurricanes; crews lose money (or worse) when the storms strike near their home bases—but then others close by, just out of the

direct path, end up making more money as the stirred-up sea floor sends the shrimp scurrying to the outside of the cyclone's edges. The faithful hang hurricane crosses made of shells in their homes, or visit churches like Key West's Basilica of St. Mary Star of the Sea, where an Our Lady of Lourdes grotto was constructed to protect against hurricanes. When a storm is headed to the Conch Republic, that's where you'll find TV film crews doing their broadcasts, and churchgoers lighting votive candles and saying the rosary. Designed in 1922 by Sister Louis Gabriel in honor of her survival through three hurricanes, there must be something to her work: There hasn't been a devastating storm on Key West since. ✤

Overleaf: Engine trouble and repairing nets aboard the *Christina Leigh*. Photos by Jay Fleming.

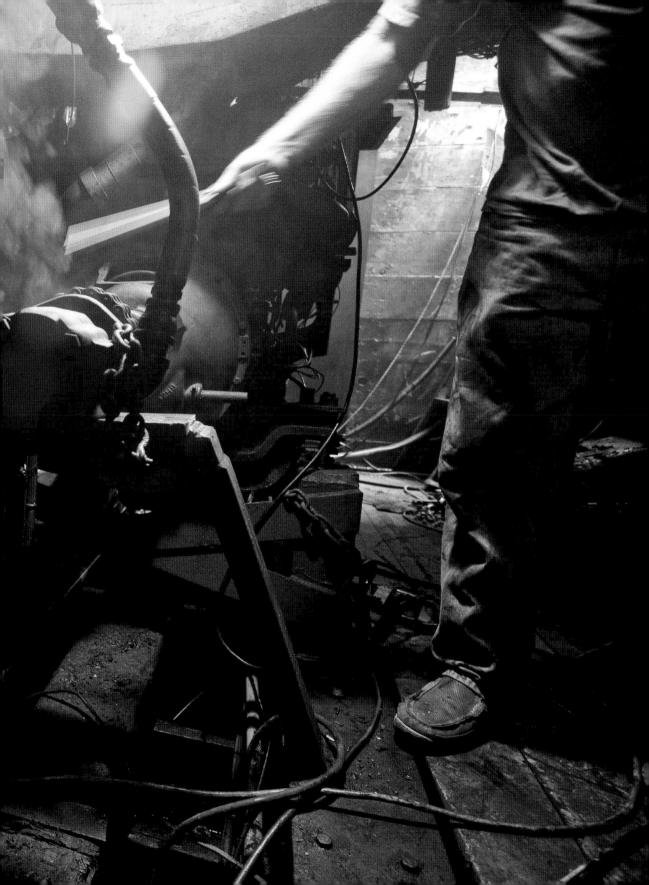

Shrimp Quiche

Jan Gregory Moore | Harkers Island, North Carolina

Harkers Island is one of the lesser-known Outer Banks refuges. It's more "primitive," according to Jan, whose family has long roots and present interests in the shrimping industry. Since it's not exactly a fine dining sort of destination, when on island, Jan whips this quiche up for brunches, lunches, and dinners. It's quick, pretty, and delicious. Enjoy it with a nice green salad, then head on back out to the beach, or to a hammock for a nap.

Serves 6 to 8

INGREDIENTS

1 (9-inch) frozen piecrust

2 large eggs, beaten

½ cup mayonnaise

2 tablespoons all-purpose flour

½ cup milk

1 pound shrimp, boiled, shelled, deveined, and cut into bite-sized pieces if large

2 cups shredded Swiss cheese

⅓ cup chopped scallions

PROCESS

1 Bake the piecrust at 400°F for 3 minutes; prick with a fork and bake for 5 minutes more. Lower the oven temperature to 350°F.

2 Combine the eggs, mayonnaise, flour, and milk; mix well. Stir in the shrimp, cheese, and scallions. Pour into the piecrust.

3 Bake for 30 minutes, or until set. Let stand for 10 minutes before serving.

Barbecued Shrimp Feast

Connie Reisinger | St. Simons Island, Georgia

Remember Rule #6: To gauge how much shrimp you'll need for your guests, assume you'll yield about half the raw weight after the shrimp is shelled and headed; each guest will eat between ½ and 1 pound of shrimp at a feast, so double the raw weight. Some folks like to leave the heads on, though, as in this recipe, because they add so much flavor.

Serves 4 to 6

INGREDIENTS

1 cup (2 sticks) butter

8 ounces margarine

6 tablespoons Worcestershire sauce

2 tablespoons freshly ground
   black pepper

½ teaspoon ground dried rosemary

2 lemons, sliced

½ teaspoon hot sauce

2 teaspoons salt

2 cloves garlic, minced

4 pounds jumbo shrimp, heads
   and tails on

PROCESS

1 Preheat the oven to 400°F.

2 Melt the butter and margarine in a saucepan. Add all the remaining ingredients except the shrimp and mix thoroughly.

3 Divide the shrimp between two shallow glass dishes and pour the heated sauce over them. Stir well.

4 Bake for 15 to 20 minutes, turning the shrimp over after 10 minutes. Serve hot.

Tasty Treasures

Gordon Lipscomb | Brownsville, Texas

Gordon Lipscomb's dynamite kebab is the kind you'll never find in a restaurant, but instead experience at a summer barbecue (and beg for the recipe on your way out). Thankfully Tony Reisinger did just that, so Gordon's saucy alchemy has been chronicled for the rest of us.

Serves 8

INGREDIENTS

48 large domestic farm-raised shrimp, shelled and deveined (about 2 pounds)

2 (12-ounce) cans of cola

¾ cup teriyaki sauce

¼ cup soy sauce

1 tablespoon Worcestershire sauce

½ cup olive oil

3 tablespoons chopped fresh cilantro

2 tablespoons minced garlic

Juice of 2 limes

1½ pounds thick-cut pepper bacon slices, cut in half

2 sweet onions, cut into chunks for kebabs

1 green or red bell pepper, cut into chunks for kebabs

PROCESS

1 Marinate the shrimp in the cola, sauces, oil, cilantro, garlic, and lime juice in a freezer bag in the refrigerator for 5 hours.

2 Soak bamboo skewers in water for 30 minutes.

3 Wrap each shrimp in a half-slice of bacon and thread 3 to 4 each of shrimp and vegetables onto the skewers, keeping all elements pushed tightly together so the skewers don't burn on the grill.

4 Prepare a hot charcoal fire.

5 Grill the kebabs over medium fire for 2 to 3 minutes, flip, and cook until the shrimp are pink and opaque. Serve immediately.

Moroccan Baked Shrimp

Nisrine Merzouki, Dinner & Dreams | www.dinnersanddreams.net

While Nisrine is based in Orlando, Florida, she honors her mother's Moroccan heritage in the kitchen with dishes like this that take advantage of the fresh shrimp available throughout the state.

Serves 4

INGREDIENTS

16 fresh cilantro sprigs

5 cloves garlic

3 tablespoons olive oil

2 tablespoons balsamic vinegar

1 tablespoon tomato paste

Grated zest of ½ lemon

Sea salt to taste

1 pound medium shrimp, peeled (leave the tails on) and deveined

Juice of 1 lemon

Hot cooked rice

Spiced Yogurt Dip (see recipe, page 44)

PROCESS

1 Preheat the oven to 325°F.

2 Process the cilantro, garlic, oil, vinegar, tomato paste, lemon zest, and salt in a food processor until smooth. Transfer to a large bowl. Add the shrimp and toss well to coat.

3 Arrange the shrimp in a single layer in a baking pan or on a cookie sheet. Bake for 10 to 12 minutes.

4 Serve the shrimp right away with lemon juice over rice and spiced yogurt dip as an accompaniment, if desired.

Shrimp Cakes à la Betty

Elizabeth Hyle Burgard | Eldersburg, Maryland

This is a play on my mother's crab cake recipe. Betty wasn't an eager chef, but then cooking every day for eight people can kind of kill the joy one might have otherwise felt. However, her crab cakes were first-rate—in the true Maryland style where you taste the crab, not fillers and extras (her secret was using the more flavorful claw meat). Mom's maternal line dates back to the 1600s in Dorchester County, Maryland; her seafood-loving Tidewater roots "willed out" through this recipe. She fried up a plate of these whenever one of us came home from some big adventure. Dinner was simply crab cakes and freshly sliced tomatoes from Dad's garden. She fried them in lots of butter in a big skillet, with a little vegetable oil to keep the butter from burning. Another of her tricks: chilling the cakes in the freezer for 30 minutes or so before frying—one of those essential tips passed down through generations.

In place of the pound of crabmeat she used, I've substituted a pound of spice-steamed shrimp pulsed a few times in a food processor to break up the meat so everything holds together. You can serve these as sandwiches or just with tomato slices.

Serves 4

INGREDIENTS

1 pound steamed shrimp, shelled and
  deveined
2 large eggs, beaten
2 to 3 tablespoons mayonnaise
¼ cup chopped fresh curly parsley
1 tablespoon yellow mustard

3 dashes Worcestershire sauce
2 slices white bread, broken up into small
  pieces
4 tablespoons butter
1 tablespoon vegetable oil

PROCESS

1 Pulse the shrimp a few times in a food processor until crumbly.

2 Mix well by hand with the eggs, mayonnaise, parsley, mustard, Worcestershire sauce, and bread, but not so much that the bread pieces dissolve into paste. Shape into ¾-inch-thick patties and put in the freezer for 30 minutes, separated with waxed paper.

3 Heat the butter and oil in a heavy skillet over medium-high heat until the butter is melted. Cook the crab cakes until both sides are browned, about 2 minutes per side, then lower the heat and cook until cooked through, an additional 10 minutes. Serve hot.

A vintage industrial shrimp steamer at the Maritime & Seafood Industry Museum in Biloxi, Mississippi.

Shrimp Mull

Judge E. C. Butts | Blythe Island, Georgia
From the Cassina Garden Club's 1937 edition of *Coastal Cookery*

Mull is an heirloom northern Georgia recipe, standing shoulder to shoulder with other regional dishes including Brunswick stew; the Lowcountry's bog, perloo, and Frogmore stew; North Carolina's muddle; and Louisiana's gumbo, Creole, and jambalaya. Mull is usually a cream stew, but this version is for a tomato broth—still thickened with cracker crumbs, as is traditional. The Cassina Garden Club on St. Simons Island has been keeping such culinary and other Sea Isle traditions vibrantly alive through their stewardship and preservation efforts since 1928.

Serves 10

INGREDIENTS

2 (14½-ounce) cans diced tomatoes

1 (10¾-ounce) can tomato soup

1 lemon, sliced

2 cloves garlic, sliced

1 cup (2 sticks) butter, divided

2 cups diced bacon

1 cup chopped onion

1 cup chopped celery

1 teaspoon celery seed

15 drops hot sauce

1 (14-ounce) bottle of ketchup

2 tablespoons Worcestershire sauce

¼ teaspoon ground allspice

¼ teaspoon curry powder

5 pounds shrimp, peeled and deveined

1 cup dry sherry

1 sleeve saltines or other mildly flavored
   and salted crackers, crushed

Hot cooked rice

Pickles

Rye bread

PROCESS

1 In a heavy stew pot, combine 2 quarts water, the tomatoes, tomato soup, lemon, and garlic.

2 Melt ½ cup of butter in a frying pan; add the bacon and onion and cook until the bacon is crisp and the onion is browned, about 10 minutes, then add to the stew pot.

3 Add the celery, celery seed, hot sauce, ketchup, Worcestershire sauce, allspice, and curry powder. Bring to a boil and simmer for 2 hours.

4 Add the shrimp; simmer for 1 hour.

5 Add ½ cup of butter, the sherry, and cracker crumbs and heat through.

6 Serve over rice in bowls, with pickles and rye bread.

Shrimp, Sausage, and Wild Rice Bog

Barbara Ambrose, Stono Market & Tomato Shed Café | Johns Island, South Carolina

Bog is an aptly named juicy Lowcountry rice casserole; chicken can be substituted for the shrimp, with sautéed sliced mushrooms added.

Serves 4

INGREDIENTS

6-ounce box mixed long-grain and wild rice

1¼ cups Shrimp Stock (see recipe, page 25)

1 cup smoked sausage cut into bite-sized pieces

¼ cup diced celery

¼ cup diced sweet onion (Vidalia or Walla Walla)

1 tablespoon chopped garlic

Butter for sautéing

2 pounds shrimp, shelled, deveined, and cut into pieces if large

PROCESS

1 Cook the rice according to the directions on the box, but replacing half of the water with shrimp stock.

2 In a sauté pan over medium heat, cook the sausage, celery, onion, and garlic in butter, stirring frequently, until the onion is translucent, 7 to 10 minutes. Add the shrimp and cook until heated through. Add the sausage, shrimp, and vegetable mixture to the cooked rice and toss to combine. Serve hot.

American Rice

From Colonial Lowcountry Beginnings, an American Power Crop Was Born

When I used to think of America's "amber waves of grain," the expanses of Kansas's wheat farms generally came to mind. Fields of rice in Arkansas, California, Louisiana, and Texas (with smaller concerns along the Mississippi and Pee Dee Rivers) never crossed my mind. Spending time in the South offered many points of education, including learning that about 85 percent of the rice we eat comes from American farms. The United States is also the fifth-largest exporter of the crop, according to the USDA. Who knew?

Historians generally agree that rice was introduced to coastal South Carolina by the start of the eighteenth century, having wended its way along colonial routes from Asia. Fifty years or so later, there were one hundred high-production plantations in the state; rice was the King of Crops long before cotton. After the Civil War, rice farming moved westward into Louisiana then onward to Texas (where farmers were given rice as a gift by the Japanese emperor) and Arkansas. At about the same time in California, the influx of about forty thousand railway-building Chinese immigrants began to plant rice fields for personal use; California is now one of the five leading producers.

Rice is at the heart of heritage Lowcountry dishes like shrimp mull (see recipe, page 188), bog (page 189), and pilau (page 213)—influenced by British colonial exposure to Near Eastern pilafs and Indian pilaus. Cajun recipes such as gumbo (page 117) and jambalaya (with its nod to West African jollof and Spanish paella) are rice-based, too. Along Texas's Gulf coast, Hispanic dishes are accompanied by rice, and in southern Florida, Cuban yellow (turmeric, garlic, and onion) rice is the accompaniment. Rice is to the South what potatoes are to the North.

Plumfield Plantation, a colonial-era farm on South Carolina's Pee Dee River, is a 25,000-acre timber and agricultural interest. Campbell Coxe, a fifth-generation farmer on the land, first planted rice in the 1990s to attract ducks and geese for hunting. "Rice is a fairly expensive crop, so I needed to make the fields pay for my hunting habit by harvesting and selling it." He now plants about two hundred acres of rice, including the variety that colonial planters made famous— Carolina Gold—working with

Beaumont, Texas, seed breeder Dr. Anna McClung. It's a classic success story, aided in no small part by none other than Martha Stewart, as Coxe tells it: "I got a call from one of Stewart's lieutenants saying they were looking for some rice to feature. I didn't know who she was, so I asked my wife if Martha was a friend of hers. She thought she married the dumbest redneck in the South!" Stewart proclaimed Coxe's Gold the best rice in America, and "then it snowballed down here in the woods."

Coxe speaks about his restoration of this rice to Carolina soil as a nearly hallowed avocation. He's as engaged and satisfied by employing modern environmental practices like using a landfill's methane gas to power the milling and packaging as he is by seeing the fields as they would have looked three hundred years ago. He'll tell you about the leggy blue herons and skulking alligators that call the diked environment home. He describes September's "halo" that forms when the temperatures of the flooded field waters and the air differ enough to create a fog bank tinged by the reflection of the golden grains. He likens the rustling of the grasses in the breeze to the sound of a taffeta ballgown skimming a hardwood floor. He'll have you picturing the flipping of the rice in the air from sweetgrass baskets (woven from local marsh grasses) that separated the rice from the chaff. It's a romantic life, but a physically demanding one. It's also commercially successful—and doesn't require the neckties that his three brothers have to put on for work. Coxe and his wife, Meredith, eat rice for breakfast, lunch, and dinner; his favorite dish is a cold shrimp and rice salad with dill on a steamy summer day.

This multibillion-dollar industry has employed an enormous number of southern (and Californian, and Arkansian) farmers, millers, and merchants since the 1700s. Hundreds of rice varieties are now grown on about ten thousand farms—including aromatics like basmati and jasmine that pair with Indian and Thai food and the starchy Arborio that's used for risottos, and many more—but each and every type has Carolina Gold as part of its ancestry. As Campbell Coxe says, "It's the granddaddy of them all."

The more I learn about rice, the more it seems like an agricultural mirror to coastal folks themselves. It's semi-aquatic, spending half its time in water. It's susceptible to insect attacks, just like southerners preyed upon by skeeters and "noseeum" sand gnats. It survives steaming from intense heat and humidity, and is both adapted to modern life and true to its traditional ways. ❖

Shrimp and Crab Casserole

Barbara Ambrose, Stono Market & Tomato Shed Café | Johns Island, South Carolina

Casseroles are a homey standby; their comfort reminds me of tea in England—able to soothe all manner of situations and wounds. I remember hearing a woman in Savannah talk about a recently widowed gentleman in her church who was on all the unmarried women's radars; her friend just about shouted: "Sugar, if that man was in *my* congregation, I'd bake him a casserole in a skinny minute!" I've no doubt this shrimp and crab casserole could open the pathway to many an unsuspecting man's heart.

Serves 4

INGREDIENTS

¼ cup diced yellow onion

¼ cup diced bell pepper (red and/or green)

Olive oil or butter for sautéing and coating the baking dish

4 cups cooked white rice

¾ cup mayonnaise

½ cup tomato sauce

12 ounces peeled and deveined medium shrimp

1 pound crabmeat, picked over to remove shells

2 tablespoons seafood boil spice

1½ cups seasoned bread crumbs

PROCESS

1 Preheat the oven to 350°F.

2 In a sauté pan over medium heat, gently cook the onion and pepper in a little oil or butter until tender, about 5 minutes.

3 Combine the onion and pepper with the rice, mayonnaise, tomato sauce, shrimp, crabmeat, and seafood boil spice and transfer to a buttered 8-inch square baking dish; top with the bread crumbs.

4 Bake for 45 minutes and serve hot.

A memorial for trawler crew members and other fishermen lost at sea, South Padre Island, Texas.

Shrimp Paesano

Texas Shrimp Association

The Texas Shrimp Association, established in 1950, supports Gulf shrimp industry folks, including fleet owners and crews. *Paesano* means a fellow villager, a friend from the neighborhood, in Italian. Here, it's a comforting dish to share with someone you love.

Serves 2

INGREDIENTS

1 pound large shrimp, peeled and
    deveined, tails left on (if preferred)
Milk (enough to cover the shrimp)
All-purpose flour for dredging
1 cup light olive oil
1 large egg yolk

Juice of 1 lemon
½ cup (1 stick) butter
1 to 2 cloves garlic, minced
Chopped fresh parsley, cilantro,
    and/or chives

PROCESS

1 Soak the shrimp in milk to cover for 5 to 10 minutes, then drain and dredge in flour.

2 Preheat the broiler to high.

3 Heat the oil in a large sauté pan over medium-high heat until hot. Add the shrimp and cook for 1 minute; be careful not to overcook the shrimp.

4 Using a slotted spoon, remove the shrimp to a rimmed baking sheet and broil for 5 minutes, or until golden brown. Drain on paper towels.

5 Combine the egg yolk and lemon juice in a heavy saucepan; add half of the butter and stir over low heat until melted. Add the remaining butter and the garlic; whisk until the butter melts and the sauce thickens.

6 Place the shrimp on a plate and top with the sauce. Sprinkle with parsley and serve.

Crispy Popcorn Shrimp
with Buttered Corn Aioli

Chef Chris Shepherd, Underbelly | Houston, Texas

James Beard Award–winning Chef Shepherd offers this special when the tender small brown bay shrimp are available, just twice a year, before they swim out to the Gulf to grow big and strong.

Serves 4 to 6

INGREDIENTS

4 ears of corn—kernels cut off and reserved, cobs reserved

½ onion, cut into four pieces

1 clove garlic, crushed

½ cup whipping cream

1 tablespoon cornstarch mixed with 1 tablespoon water

¾ cup plus 2 tablespoons Butter Buds

Kosher salt and freshly ground black pepper

1 cup rice flour

1 large egg

½ cup whole milk

1 pound small shrimp, shelled and deveined

Vegetable oil for frying

PROCESS

1 In a large saucepan, combine the corn cobs with the onion, garlic, and 6 cups water and bring to a boil. Simmer over medium-low heat, stirring occasionally, until the broth is well flavored and reduced down to about 2 cups, about 40 minutes. Strain the broth into a heatproof bowl, discarding the solids.

2 Return the broth to the saucepan and bring to a boil. Simmer over medium heat until reduced to 1 cup, 7 to 10 minutes. Add the corn kernels and cream and bring just to a boil, then stir in the cornstarch mixture and simmer over medium heat until thickened, about 3 minutes.

3 Transfer the mixture to a blender and puree until smooth. Strain the puree through a medium-mesh sieve set over a bowl. Stir in the imitation butter powder and season the sauce with salt and pepper; keep warm.

4 Set a rack over a baking sheet. Put the rice flour in a pie plate. In another pie plate, beat the egg together with the milk. Season the shrimp with salt and pepper and dredge them in the rice flour, tapping off the excess. Dip the shrimp in the egg, then dredge again in the flour; transfer to the rack.

5 In a large saucepan, heat 1½ inches of oil to 350°F. Add half of the shrimp to the oil and fry until golden and crisp, about 2 minutes. Using a slotted spoon, transfer the shrimp to a paper towel–lined baking sheet and season lightly with salt and pepper. Repeat with the remaining shrimp. Serve hot.

Gambas al Ajillo (Shrimp in Garlic Sauce)

Chef Kurtis Schumm, Tybee Island Social Club | Tybee Island, Georgia

Chef Schumm recommends kissing as many people as possible after eating this delicious, garlicky dish.

Serves 4

INGREDIENTS

½ cup olive oil

1 baguette, sliced

¾ cup (1½ sticks) unsalted butter

20 medium cloves garlic, peeled

2 pounds large (21- to 25-count) shrimp, heads and shells on, shells split along the back

¼ cup paprika

1 cup dry sherry

Salt and freshly ground black pepper to taste

½ cup chopped fresh flat-leaf parsley

2 lemons, sliced

PROCESS

1 Heat a 10-inch or larger cast-iron skillet over medium-high heat and add the oil.

2 When oil is hot, briefly fry the sliced baguette on both sides and then set aside.

3 In the same skillet, add the butter (it's good to keep a lid or piece of aluminum foil nearby in case it splatters).

4 Once the butter is lightly browned, add the garlic, paprika, and sherry. Cook until the sauce is reduced by two thirds, about 10 minutes.

5 Add the shrimp and toss to coat with the sauce; cook for 4 to 5 minutes, until pink, then sprinkle with salt and pepper.

6 Divide the shrimp among four serving bowls. Garnish with parsley and lemon slices and serve with the toasted bread for dipping.

Jamaican Jerk Shrimp

Shaggy's | Pass Christian, Mississippi

When I first walked into Shaggy's in Pass Christian, I saw a guy drinking at the bar on a fishing boat's bench seat with the rod holders along the back. The restaurant is right on the docks, where trawlers and lots of other boats are lined up; you can buy fresh shrimp at a stand right next to them, or sit yourself down inside and enjoy these jerk shrimp and lots of other tasty offerings.

Serves 2

INGREDIENTS

12 large (21- to 25-count) shrimp, peeled and deveined

2 tablespoons Caribbean jerk seasoning

2 tablespoons olive oil

1 tablespoon unsalted butter

1 cup sugar

½ cup soy sauce

1 cup cooked rice

½ cup sweet chili sauce

Juice of 1 lime

PROCESS

1 Toss the shrimp in the jerk seasoning.

2 Heat the oil and butter in a sauté pan over medium-high heat; add the shrimp and cook for 2 minutes per side, or until pink and the tails have curled in.

3 To make the soy glaze, combine the sugar and soy sauce in a small saucepan. Bring to almost a boil, then reduce the heat to a simmer. Do not allow it to boil—it will overflow. Cook until thickened into a glaze, about 5 minutes.

4 Place the sautéed shrimp on top of the cooked rice on a platter. Drizzle with sweet chili sauce and some of the soy glaze while hot. Squeeze the lime juice on top. Serve immediately. Refrigerate any remaining soy glaze for up to 1 week, using it for other broiled and grilled chicken and seafood dishes.

Mississippi's Gulf Coast has a strong commitment to public art, including sculptures made from hurricane-decimated live oak trees, bronze plaques of local wildlife dotting the bridges along Beach Boulevard, and this work by Marty Wilson that salutes the area's shrimping heritage.

Shrimp Scampi

I've played with this recipe lo, these last fifteen years or more. It wasn't until very recently that I added the lemon zest, though, which makes a big difference. This is also great with an equivalent amount of chicken tenders cut up into bite-sized pieces and marinated the same way. I cook this for my friend Dave's dinners to benefit a local theater group; as an appetizer, he serves three shrimp with a grilled piece of baguette in a ramekin or on a plate.

Serves 4

INGREDIENTS

1 teaspoon dried oregano

2 teaspoons dried basil

1¼ pounds large shrimp, shelled and deveined

¼ cup olive oil

4 tablespoons butter, melted and cooled

2 teaspoons minced garlic, or to taste

2 tablespoons chopped fresh curly parsley

1 tablespoon pickled jalapeño brine

6 large pickled jalapeño slices, finely chopped

2 tablespoons Italian bread crumbs

½ teaspoon freshly ground black pepper

½ teaspoon salt

Grated zest of 1 lemon

2 cups hot cooked basmati rice

Dry white wine

PROCESS

1 Crush the oregano and basil in a plastic sandwich bag with the back of a spoon to release their oils.

2 Combine the herbs and all the remaining ingredients except the rice and wine until the shrimp are well coated; cover and refrigerate overnight.

3 Take the shrimp mixture out of the refrigerator about 1 hour before serving.

4 Spread the rice on a serving platter.

5 Sauté the shrimp quickly in a wok or large, heavy pan (not nonstick). Remove the shrimp to the rice platter.

6 Deglaze the pan with the wine, just enough to release the cooked-on sauce; drizzle on top of the shrimp.

Photo by Charity Burggraaf.

Shrimp Saganaki

Patrice Berry, Circle B Kitchen | www.circle-b-kitchen.com

I first encountered shrimp saganaki in Tarpon Springs, Florida, which was built mainly by Greek immigrant sponge divers and merchants. It's the only place in the country where you can legally harvest sponges by diving for them (you can spear for them in the Keys). Sponge shops line the streets, and you still hear conversations in Greek. I couldn't wrestle a recipe from the restaurant I visited, but Patrice Berry was kind enough to share her delicious take on the dish.

Serves 2

INGREDIENTS

3 tablespoons olive oil

½ small red onion, sliced

½ green bell pepper, sliced

½ yellow or red bell pepper, sliced

2 ripe tomatoes, diced (about 1 cup)

½ cup kalamata olives, sliced

1 teaspoon dried Greek oregano

½ teaspoon red pepper flakes (or more
   to taste)

1 cup marinara (or tomato) sauce

½ cup Greek feta cheese, coarsely
   crumbled (plus a little more for the top)

Splash of ouzo (or add ¼ teaspoon
   ground fennel and a splash of vodka to
   the sauce)

Salt to taste

12 large shrimp, peeled and deveined,
   tails left on

1 tablespoon chopped fresh oregano

Crusty bread

PROCESS

1 Preheat the broiler to high.

2 In a medium skillet, heat the oil over medium-high heat, then add the onion, bell peppers, tomatoes, olives, dried oregano, and red pepper flakes. Sauté until the onion is soft and the tomatoes are starting to break down, 5 to 7 minutes.

3 Add the marinara sauce and simmer for 5 to 10 minutes, until a thick sauce forms.

4 Stir in the cheese and ouzo. Taste and adjust the seasoning with salt (if required) and additional red pepper flakes (if desired) and arrange the shrimp on top.

5 Sprinkle the remaining cheese on top, and place under the broiler for about 5 minutes, or until the shrimp are cooked through.

6 Sprinkle with the fresh oregano and serve with crusty bread.

Facing: Photo by Charity Burggraaf.

Overleaf: Docks in Tarpon Springs, Florida, are lined not only with shrimp trawlers but also sponge divers' boats.

Cherry Point Shrimp and Rice

Jane LaRoche | Rockville, South Carolina

The LaRoche family has been netting and cooking shrimp for hundreds of years in Rockville, a village that seems untouched by time and is home to the Sea Island Yacht Club, host of a 120-year heritage regatta that's always the last race of the sailing season. This is their take on the shrimp 'n' gravy dish that's so commonly rustled up by folks in the shrimping industry.

Serves 8

INGREDIENTS

4 slices bacon

1 small onion, finely chopped

1 bell pepper, chopped

2 cups cooked rice

2 pounds shelled and deveined shrimp

2 tablespoons Worcestershire sauce

All-purpose flour for dredging

4 tablespoons butter

Salt and freshly ground black pepper
  to taste

PROCESS

1 Fry the bacon in a skillet until crisp, then drain on paper towels, reserving 2 to 3 tablespoons of drippings in the skillet.

2 Sauté the onion and bell pepper in the drippings until tender, 3 to 5 minutes.

3 Toss the shrimp in the Worcestershire sauce.

4 Dredge the shrimp in flour to coat.

5 Melt the butter in a large sauté pan; add the shrimp in a single layer and cook over medium-low heat for about 3 minutes, until the shrimp are golden on the bottom; turn and brown on the other side.

6 Add the rice, sautéed vegetables, and crumbled bacon slices to the pan with the shrimp, tossing until well mixed. Season with salt and pepper to taste and serve.

Sea Island Yacht Club's annual Rockville Regatta—which recently celebrated its 125th anniversary—closes the sailing season on Bohicket Creek, South Carolina. Photo by Brenda Gilliam.

A Prince among Pirates

Captain Antoine Gilliard, the *Tina Marie*, Rockville, South Carolina

The LaRoche family has pulled shrimp, flounder, wreckfish, and other delicacies from Bohicket Creek and its surrounding tidal waters for centuries; theirs was the first home built in Rockville. They've also owned Cherry Point Seafood since 1933, so they've encountered their share of Lowcountry captains and crews. Daniel LaRoche likens most of them to rogues: "There aren't many opportunities left to be your own boss, work as much or as little as you want, and not have to get along with anyone else—there's a lot of freedom in that. Most of the guys don't want to play by any rules: Very few have drivers' licenses, bank accounts, or phones. They're both suspicious and mischievous by nature, but they function." In the end, all that matters is showing up on the dock before the boat leaves, hauling in the fish, and bringing the boat back in one piece.

Having said all that, however, when LaRoche talks about Antoine Gilliard

and his father, Arthur, who both run trawlers for the family, it's clear that there are exceptions in the off-the-grid collection of mariners. "Antoine is better suited to society than most of us—he's just more normal. He's respectful and has a strong work ethic, and his heart's in it, too."

Antoine will tell you he's no Boy Scout; for one thing, he cusses, well, like a sailor: "I have a pretty filthy mouth after a life around shrimpers." But his daddy taught him right, ever since he was eleven and stood on a milk crate to watch the wheel while his dad slept. He was itchin' to work when he was even younger: "When I was a little kid, I jumped on boats with a needle offerin' to fix peoples' nets." He was a captain by the tender age of seventeen. His dad taught him how to run his crews by being patient, by treating the men as he'd want to be treated. "You live with these guys on the boat; you're one family. You don't turn your back on them." His father also drilled into him to look first and think before he acts. "There are accidents waitin' to happen out there and I don't want anyone to get hurt. They tell me if anyone else was runnin' the *Tina Marie*, she woulda been sunk a long time ago."

Antoine is now thirty-five and has seen his share of great hauls, terrifying

storms that rock and roll the boat with forty-mile-per-hour winds, bloody accidents, strange objects caught in the nets, and all the rest that comes with the job. He knows how hard it is to keep his mind right after thirteen hours of holding a twisted rudder in position by hand. The missing part of a finger reminds him how dangerous it all can be, but what he's most proud of is that he and his dad are two of maybe a handful of black trawler captains on the East Coast. Black, white, or Asian, Antoine is one of the best in the business. ❧

Shrimp de Grill

Chef George Spriggs, North Beach Grill | Tybee Island, Georgia

North Beach Grill sits next to Fort Screven and in front of Tybee's beautifully restored lighthouse complex, a shell's throw from the dunes. Its bright colors, screened windows, and open deck invite barefooted guests to relax, watch the squadrons of pelicans fly by, and listen to the reggae. Everything on the menu is fantastic; Chef Spriggs serves this dish at more formal catered events on the island, in Savannah, and throughout the region.

Serves 4

INGREDIENTS

2 tablespoons olive oil

1 pound large shrimp, peeled and deveined

1 tablespoon chopped garlic

¼ cup Pernod (or other licorice-flavored liqueur)

2 tablespoons butter

½ cup thinly sliced dried apricots

1 teaspoon cracked black pepper

Hot cooked rice

PROCESS

1 Place a sauté pan over high heat and allow to heat for about 1 minute. Add the oil, followed by the shrimp. Toss or stir the shrimp until pink coloring begins to appear, then add the garlic.

2 Continue to toss the shrimp for 30 seconds, then add the Pernod. Once the Pernod is added, the pan should catch fire to burn off the alcohol. If it doesn't, light the dish with a long-handled lighter. Cook until the liquid is reduced by half.

3 Add the butter and dried apricots. Continue to toss. Add the cracked pepper and toss.

4 Serve over rice.

Shrimp Pilau

Campbell Coxe, Carolina Plantation Rice | Darlington, South Carolina

Pilau is a centuries-old Lowcountry recipe that's also known as "perloo" and is related to pilafs, which are actually of Indian lineage, brought along by English colonists. Carolina Plantation Rice's golden variety is a beautiful choice for this dish (for more about American rice, heirloom and otherwise, see page 190).

Serves 6 to 8

INGREDIENTS

6 to 8 slices bacon, or 8 ounces loose
  sausage (hot or regular)
2 cups uncooked golden rice
3 tablespoons butter, or more if desired
1 cup chopped celery
½ cup chopped bell pepper
3 cups shrimp, peeled and deveined

2 tablespoons all-purpose flour
2 teaspoons Worcestershire sauce
Salt and freshly ground black pepper
  to taste
Hot sauce to taste (optional)
½ cup chopped fresh parsley
1 cup diced tomatoes

PROCESS

1 Fry the bacon until crisp, then drain on paper towels and crumble; reserve the drippings. (If using sausage, cook it until browned and reserve the drippings.)

2 Cook the rice according to the directions on the package, adding bacon or sausage drippings to the cooking water.

3 In a heavy skillet or saucepan, melt the butter; add the celery and bell pepper. Sauté for a few minutes; add the shrimp and stir and simmer for about 5 minutes, until the shrimp is cooked through; sprinkle in the flour and mix well.

4 Add the Worcestershire sauce, salt and pepper, and hot sauce, if desired.

5 Add the rice to the shrimp and stir until well blended. Add more butter, if desired, and stir in the crumbled bacon or sausage and fresh parsley.

6 Transfer to a serving platter and sprinkle the tomatoes on top.

Teriyaki Shrimp

Annette Reddell Hegen from *Hooked on Seafood*, created for
Texas A&M's Sea Grant Program

Hegen suggests packing the marinating shrimp in ice and cooking them over an open campfire—but a wok in a kitchen will do nicely, too! Mild fish filets like tilapia or swai can be substituted for the shrimp.

Serves 4 to 6

INGREDIENTS

2 pounds shrimp, peeled and deveined

½ cup soy sauce

½ cup rice wine (sake)

3 cloves garlic, minced

¼ cup sugar

1 teaspoon grated fresh ginger

Vegetable oil for stir-frying

Hot cooked rice

PROCESS

1 Put all the ingredients in a plastic freezer bag; seal and refrigerate for at least 2 hours.

2 Remove the shrimp and cook by grilling on skewers or stir-frying in a bit of oil in a wok or high-sided pan over high heat.

3 Serve over rice.

Coastal roads throughout the South are dotted with wildlife protection signs, including those for crocodiles in Key West, Florida; turtles on Tybee Island, Georgia; and here on South Padre Island, Texas, pelicans.

seven

Go Withs

Side Dishes

Summer and fall parties in the South are visions of tables spread wide and deep with all sorts of savory and sweet delights; it's hard to go wrong with any accompaniment for a shrimp feast, Lowcountry boil, shrimp kebabs, or other shrimp dishes. Here are some stars that I was raised on, along with others gathered from our shrimp country's many shores and lanes.

The beach at Botany Bay Plantation Heritage Preserve on Edisto Island, South Carolina.

Polenta Cakes

Chef Antonio Galan, Galvez Bar & Grill | Galveston, Texas

Chef Galan serves these with his Shrimp and Polenta, but you can use the cakes for Shrimp Benedict (page 126) and for many other dishes, too. If you like crispier cakes, mix ⅓ cup Italian bread crumbs and ⅔ cup panko bread crumbs and dredge the cakes in the mixture before panfrying.

Serves 4 to 6

INGREDIENTS

4½ cups chicken stock

1¾ cups instant polenta

2 red bell peppers, finely diced

1 green bell pepper, finely diced

½ cup (1 stick) butter

1 cup crumbled feta cheese

Olive oil

PROCESS

1 Bring the stock to a boil in a stock pot. Add the polenta and peppers, whisking constantly until the liquid begins to bubble up.

2 When the polenta is thick and the grains are tender, remove from the heat and whisk in the butter, then fold in the cheese. Spoon into a greased loaf pan and let cool, then cover and refrigerate until cold.

3 Cut the chilled polenta into ½-inch-thick slabs, then cut into triangles or other shapes with biscuit or cookie cutters.

4 Brush with oil and fry in a heavy skillet or broil until crisp. Serve hot.

Creamy Grits with Bacon

Chef Fred Neuville, Fat Hen | Johns Island, South Carolina

There are so many ways to season and cook grits—everyone has their favorite. Chef Neuville's take can be used for shrimp and grits, or as a side along with any number of main courses. It can also just be eaten all by its lonesome if you need some comfort.

Serves 4 to 6

INGREDIENTS

2 quarts Shrimp Stock (see recipe, page 25)

4½ cups half-and-half

2 cups grits

1½ cups grated Parmesan cheese

4 ounces bacon, cooked until crisp, crumbled

Freshly ground black pepper to taste

PROCESS

1 In a large pot, bring the stock and half-and-half to a boil over high heat. Reduce the heat to simmer and add the grits. Cook over medium heat, stirring frequently, until the grits thicken up with no lumps, 10 to 12 minutes.

2 Add the cheese and whisk until nice and smooth.

3 Add the bacon and pepper until the seasoning suits you (the cheese will add all the salt you need). Serve hot.

Savory Rice

Chef Fred Neuville, Fat Hen | Johns Island, South Carolina

This can be paired with just about anything from grilled steaks to kebabs to broiled fish. You can also toss in a pound of shrimp and/or sausage and chicken to make it a main course.

Makes 1 1/2 cups

INGREDIENTS

4 strips applewood-smoked bacon, diced

½ yellow onion, diced

1 tablespoon butter

½ cup uncooked long-grain rice

¼ cup minced scallions

1 tablespoon fresh lemon juice

Hot sauce (start with 1 tablespoon and adjust to taste)

Salt and freshly ground black pepper (optional)

PROCESS

1 Cook the bacon and onion in a saucepan over medium heat until the onion is tender, about 4 minutes; do not brown. Add the butter and cook until melted.

2 Add the rice and cook, stirring, for 30 seconds.

3 Add water to cover the rice by about 1 inch.

4 Bring to a boil, then lower the heat and cook until all the liquid is absorbed and the rice is tender, about 10 minutes.

5 Stir in the scallions, lemon juice, and hot sauce. Add salt and pepper to taste, if desired.

Overleaf: "The water is wide, I cannot get o'er. And neither have I the wings to fly. Build me a boat that can carry two, And both shall row, my love and I." Bohicket Creek, South Carolina.

Deviled Eggs

Deviled eggs are like pizza or nachos for me—even when they're not great, they're good. This recipe is a fancier version of the traditional mayonnaise and mustard mix that presents well for parties. Or binge television sessions. Or because it's Tuesday.

Makes 24 egg halves

INGREDIENTS

1 dozen eggs, boiled, peeled, and cut in half lengthwise, yolks set aside

3 tablespoons Rémoulade (see recipe, page 31)

1 tablespoon sour cream or plain yogurt

4 ounces medium steamed shrimp

3 dashes of hot sauce

Small sprigs fresh curly parsley or dill

Paprika or seafood boil spice

PROCESS

1 Combine the cooked egg yolks, rémoulade, sour cream, and the hot sauce in a food processor until a smooth paste forms.

2 Place the filling in a quart-sized plastic sandwich bag; snip off a corner to create a piping bag and fill the egg white halves with the yolk mixture.

3 Cut the shrimp into small pieces and top each egg half with a piece of shrimp and a parsley sprig. Sprinkle with paprika. Save any remaining filling for shrimpy egg salad sandwiches, or serve with crackers.

Tip: If you don't have a deviled egg plate and need to transport these slippery devils, bunch up tin foil in a rimmed baking sheet and make indentations for the 24 egg halves to keep them from sliding, then cover with plastic wrap.

Pimento Cheese Spread

Pimento cheese is a standby tailgating and party dip and school lunch ingredient. Try it for a grilled cheese sammie, too—and throw caution completely out the back door by adding in some crisp bacon or country ham, sliced thin and seared, between the bread. Schmeer it on bagels at brunch, slather it on hot biscuits, or dig into it with celery sticks and strike a defiant pose. It won't help you reach a goal weight, but it sure will make your mouth happy. There are scores and scores of ways to make this spread; this is mine—feel free to experiment.

Makes about 3 cups

INGREDIENTS

⅔ cup mayonnaise

4 ounces cream cheese, softened

2 cups finely shredded extra-sharp cheddar cheese

1 (8-ounce) jar pimentos, drained and diced

2 tablespoons minced pickled banana pepper rings

1 teaspoon grated sweet onion, with juice

½ teaspoon garlic powder

½ teaspoon sugar

PROCESS

1 Combine all the ingredients in a bowl and refrigerate, covered, overnight.

2 Bring back to room temperature before serving with crackers or on toast points, or whatever your tongue desires.

Stono Market & Tomato Shed Café's take on pimento cheese, Johns Island, South Carolina.

Southern Street Corn

Chef Ari Kolender, Leon's Oyster Shop | Charleston, South Carolina

I hope no one was watching when Chef Kolender introduced me to this flavor explosion. I'm pretty sure I made a spectacle of myself, it's that good . . . well worth the butter bath your fingers and face take while eating it.

Makes 8 ears of corn

INGREDIENTS

½ cup (1 stick) butter, softened

½ cup mayonnaise

½ cup sour cream

1½ teaspoons hot sauce

2 tablespoons minced shallot

1½ teaspoons fresh lemon juice

1½ tablespoons seafood boil spice

8 ears of corn, shucked

Olive oil

4 cups ground fried shallots (see Note)

PROCESS

1 Prepare a hot charcoal fire.

2 In a bowl, whisk together the butter, mayonnaise, sour cream, hot sauce, shallot, lemon juice, and seafood boil spice.

3 Rub the ears of corn with oil and place them on the grill. Cook, rotating the ears occasionally, until the corn is tender and is well charred in spots.

4 Take a few spoonfuls of the butter mixture and place it in a bowl with one ear of corn at a time; toss until the corn is well coated.

5 Roll the corn in the fried shallots. Repeat with the remaining ears of corn and serve.

Note: You can find fried shallots at your local Asian market, or you can fry them yourself: Toss thinly sliced shallots in rice flour, shake them free of excess, then deep-fry them in vegetable oil at 325°F until golden. Using a slotted spoon or sieve, remove to paper towels to drain and cool. Grind the fried shallots into a crumble, and set aside.

Squash Fritters

Mrs. A. C. Hartridge | St. Simons Island, Georgia
From the Cassina Garden Club's 1937 edition of *Coastal Cookery*

Here's a yummy way to use squash from your garden when it starts to take over.

Serves 4

INGREDIENTS

1 large egg, separated

½ cup whipping cream

1 cup cooked yellow squash or zucchini, squeezed of excess water

Pinch of salt

½ teaspoon baking powder

All-purpose flour, just enough to bind into stiff batter

Canola or vegetable oil (or shortening) for deep frying

PROCESS

1 Beat the egg yolk in a medium bowl, then stir in the cream and squash.

2 Add the salt and baking powder, then add flour gradually, mixing until a stiff batter forms. Beat until smooth.

3 In a separate bowl, whisk the egg white until firm peaks form, then fold it into the batter.

4 In a heavy pot, heat 2 inches of oil to 350°F. Drop the squash mixture into the oil by spoonfuls and fry to a delicate brown, turning if necessary, 2 to 4 minutes.

5 Drain on paper towels and serve hot.

Cheddar Cream Biscuits

There are few things better than a cream biscuit hot out of the oven, but I love the process of making them almost as much as eating them. The satiny flour and silky butter being rubbed together is a kind of meditation. If a southern girl can't make a good biscuit, they take her passport away.

You can make up the dough, cut out the biscuits, and freeze them uncooked between waxed paper pieces in airtight containers to have them for emergencies. I've adapted this recipe for pot pie topping, pressing the dough out to a much thinner piece, using cookie cutters for the shapes, and arranging them on top of a casserole or thickened-up stew. I also make a sweet version, leaving out the mustard and cheese and adding 1½ teaspoons caraway seeds and 1 cup currants, and increasing the flour by ¼ to ½ cup.

Makes 20 small biscuits

INGREDIENTS

2 cups all-purpose flour, plus additional for kneading

1 tablespoon baking powder

½ teaspoon English mustard powder

½ teaspoon salt

4 tablespoons cold unsalted butter, cut into small cubes

1 cup finely grated extra-sharp cheddar cheese

1 cup whipping cream

PROCESS

1 Preheat the oven to 425°F and place a rack in the center of the oven. Lightly grease a baking sheet or cut parchment paper to fit.

2 Whisk the flour, baking powder, mustard powder, and salt together in a bowl.

3 Rub the butter into the flour until it becomes crumbly.

4 Stir in the cheese with a fork, then add the cream.

5 Knead a few times in the bowl until the dough holds together as a ball.

6 Press the dough out on a floured surface until it's ½ inch thick.

7 Cut biscuits with a small cutter and place on the prepared baking sheet 1 inch apart; gather scraps and cut additional biscuits.

8 Bake for 10 to 12 minutes, until golden but not brown.

9 Cool on a wire rack. Try not to eat them all before guests arrive.

Fried Green Tomatoes

Chef Matthew Raiford, The Hunting Lodge | Little St. Simons Island, Georgia

Fried Green Tomatoes is more than a fantastic film; it's an iconic southern side dish. They stand on their own, but Chef Raiford serves them with his Roasted Red Pepper Aioli. Fried green tomato sandwiches are not out of the question; try pairing them with goat cheese scraped across the bread.

Serves 4

INGREDIENTS

2 green tomatoes, sliced into 8 rounds,
   each ¼ to ½ inch thick

1 cup buttermilk

2 cups unsweetened corn flakes

2 large eggs

1 cup milk

4 tablespoons blackening seasoning

1 cup all-purpose flour

Canola oil for shallow-frying

Roasted Red Pepper Aioli (see recipe,
   page 30)

1 tablespoon snipped fresh curly parsley

PROCESS

1 Put the tomatoes in a glass baking dish, cover them with the buttermilk, cover the dish, and let them sit overnight in the refrigerator.

2 Grind the corn flakes in a food processor until fine.

3 In a bowl, beat the eggs and milk together.

4 In a separate bowl, whisk the blackening seasoning and the flour together.

5 Shake each slice of tomato free of excess buttermilk, then press each side in the flour mixture; coat evenly.

6 Dip the slices in the egg wash, then press into the ground cornflakes.

7 In a heavy pan, heat 1 to 2 inches of oil to 350°F. Working in batches, fry the tomato slices until browned on each side, about 4 minutes total, then drain on paper towels.

8 Drizzle the aioli over the slices, garnish with the parsley, and serve hot.

Sweet Honey Jalapeño Cheddar Cornbread

Tieghan Gerard, Half Baked Harvest | www.halfbakedharvest.com

This recipe goes with Tieghan's Spicy Beer and Butter Shrimp with Cornbread Crouton Salad (see recipe, page 118), but it's so good, you should try it with lots of other meals, too!

Serves 8

INGREDIENTS

1½ cups all-purpose flour

1½ cups cornmeal

5 teaspoons baking powder

½ teaspoon baking soda

½ teaspoon salt

½ teaspoon freshly ground black pepper

¾ cup (1½ sticks) cold unsalted butter, cut into small cubes, plus more for the baking dish

¾ cup buttermilk

1 large egg, lightly beaten

¼ cup honey

¾ cup diced sharp cheddar cheese

2 jalapeños, seeded and membranes removed (if jalapeños are small, use 3)

PROCESS

1 Preheat the oven to 425°F. Grease an 8-inch square baking dish.

2 In a large bowl, combine the flour, cornmeal, baking powder, baking soda, salt, and black pepper. Whisk until combined.

3 Using a fork, pastry blender, or your hands, add the butter to the flour and mix until coarse little crumbles remain.

4 In a separate bowl, whisk together the buttermilk, egg, and honey, and pour into the flour mixture. Stir with a spoon until just combined, not overmixing. Use your hands if needed to bring the dough together.

5 Fold in the cheese and jalapeños.

6 Press the dough into the prepared baking dish.

7 Bake for 20 to 25 minutes, until a toothpick inserted in the center comes out clean. Let cool before slicing.

Sweet Cornbread

Chef Adam Miller, Amen Street Fish & Raw Bar | Charleston, South Carolina

This is a moist, sweet version of cornbread that pairs beautifully with the spice and textures of Chef Miller's Blackened Shrimp with Black-Eyed Pea Vinaigrette (see recipe, page 91), but it's great as a breakfast bread, too, or as a side for steamed shrimp or a host of other foods.

Makes 18 to 24 pieces

INGREDIENTS

1½ cups cornmeal

1½ cups all-purpose flour

1¼ cups sugar

1 tablespoon baking powder

1 teaspoon baking soda

1 teaspoon kosher salt

3 cups buttermilk

6 large eggs

¾ cup (1½ sticks) butter, melted

PROCESS

1 In a large bowl, combine all the dry ingredients.

2 In a separate bowl, combine all the wet ingredients.

3 Mix the wet ingredients into the dry, being careful not to overmix.

4 Spray a 9-by-11-inch baking pan with cooking spray; pour the batter into the pan.

5 Bake at 350°F for 50 to 60 minutes, rotating the pan after 30 minutes. The cornbread is done when a toothpick inserted in the center comes out clean.

Black-Eyed Pea Vinaigrette Salad

Chef Adam Miller, Amen Street Fish & Raw Bar | Charleston, South Carolina

Black-eyed peas are a southern staple (by way of West Africa), served for good luck as the first thing to be eaten on New Year's Day. Some will tell you that you have to eat exactly 365 peas to get the right amount of lucky days in the new year. There's lots of lore and lots of history to these lowly legumes. If you have store-bought red pepper jelly or relish, you could take a shortcut and start at the shallots, skipping the first two steps of the directions. But having a batch of Amen Street's jam on hand is always a good thing.

Makes 7 cups

INGREDIENTS

6 roasted red bell peppers, peeled, seeds and membranes removed

2 jalapeños, seeds and membranes removed

1 small onion, roughly chopped

6 garlic cloves, peeled; plus 2 teaspoons minced

1 cup sugar

2 cups red wine vinegar

2 tablespoons finely minced shallot

2 teaspoons minced garlic

2 teaspoons mixed fresh herbs

¼ cup honey

2 cups extra-virgin olive oil

4 cups cooked black-eyed peas

Salt and freshly ground black pepper to taste

PROCESS

1 To make the red pepper jam, process the red peppers, jalapeños, onion, and whole garlic cloves in a food processor.

2 Transfer to a saucepan, stir in the sugar and 1 cup of the vinegar, and simmer until thickened and jamlike, being careful not to scorch the bottom.

3 In a medium bowl, whisk together the shallot, minced garlic, herbs, honey, the remaining 1 cup vinegar, and the oil.

4 Add 2 tablespoons red pepper jam and the black-eyed peas and season with salt and pepper; toss well. Allow to sit for 1 hour or so before serving.

Betty's Dill Pickle Potato Salad

Elizabeth Hyle Burgard | Eldersburg, Maryland

This salad was a staple at our family's summer parties, along with my dad's grilled chicken and sliced tomatoes from the garden. When we were lucky enough to have crab feasts or shrimp boils, it was also on the table. If you heard the squeak of the refrigerator door later that night, you knew someone was snacking on the leftovers!

Serves 10 to 12

INGREDIENTS

5 pounds waxy potatoes (such as Yukon gold), peeled and cut into bite-sized pieces

2 cups mayonnaise

6 tablespoons dill pickle juice

10 dill pickle spears, diced

2 teaspoons celery seed

PROCESS

1 Put the potatoes in a large pot and add cold water to cover by 4 to 5 inches.

2 Place over high heat and bring to a boil, then reduce to a soft rolling boil. Boil for 15 to 20 minutes, until a fork inserted through a cube meets only mild resistance. Don't overcook, or you'll end up with mashed potatoes instead.

3 Drain the potatoes in a colander, running cold water over them to stop the cooking. Transfer to a large bowl or serving dish.

4 In a large bowl, whisk the mayonnaise, pickle juice, pickles, and celery seed until the dressing is well combined.

5 Add the drained potatoes to the dressing and toss gently so the dressing coats the potatoes without breaking them apart. Cover and refrigerate for at least 4 hours before serving to allow the flavors to meld.

Overleaf: Snead's Ferry, North Carolina, trawlers try their luck through an inky night. Photo by Jay Fleming.

Acknowledgments

The gathering of *Shrimp Country*'s recipes and images drew me across 3,300 salty miles in September 2014. It was a trip of a lifetime—one that wouldn't have been nearly as fun, rewarding, or comfortable without the generosity of kind-hearted southerners who opened their kitchens, homes, and minds. They welcomed me in as one of their own.

To my parents, who drove me and my brother, Peter, and sister, Denise, down the coast to Emerald Isle, North Carolina, my thanks for the introduction to steamed shrimp piled on tables with ocean views.

For the joy that comes from lovingly prepared meals, my gratitude to the owners, chefs, and staffs of scores of coastal restaurants, many of which are featured in these pages through the delicious recipes they so generously lent.

Many thanks to my welcoming hosts, including Schlitterbahn Beach Resort on South Padre Island, Texas; the Omni Hotel in Corpus Christi, Texas (and Ashley Simper, guide extraordinaire); Hotel Galvez in Galveston, Texas; Stephen Hammond and Jonathon Beyers in Key West, Florida; The Lodge at Little St. Simons Island in Georgia; James Reid in Savannah, Georgia; Leuveda Garner on Tybee Island, Georgia; Carol and Lisa Hayes on Myrtle Island, South Carolina; Brenda Gilliam in Charleston, South Carolina, and Marc and Regina Burgard in Ocean City, Maryland.

To the marine biologists and historians who shared their knowledge, including Tony Reisinger on South Padre Island; Murphy Givens in Corpus Christi; Dr. Joseph Richardson on Tybee Island and Dr. Val Husley of Biloxi, Mississippi, my gratitude for the education and the storytelling.

Thanks to the team at the University Press of Florida, including Sian Hunter, Marthe Walters, Liana Krissoff, and Larry Leshan for their enthusiasm, support, and careful eyes.

And, to end where it all begins: to the shrimp trawler fleet owners and their captains and crews along the Gulf of Mexico and the Atlantic, my thanks for your candor, humor, and patience—and for braving scorching sun and tropical storms so the rest of us can feast on the bounty you shepherd to shore.

Index